**WILTSHIRE LIBRARY
& MUSEUM SERVICE**

Headquarters : Bythesea Road, Trowbridge.

Items should be returned to the library from which they
were borrowed on or before the date stamped above,
unless a renewal has been granted.   LM6.108.1

A Charm of Words

A Charm of Words

ESSAYS AND PAPERS ON LANGUAGE

BY

ERIC PARTRIDGE

HAMISH HAMILTON

LONDON

First published in Great Britain, 1960
by Hamish Hamilton Ltd.
90 Great Russell Street, London, W.C.1
© *1960 by Eric Partridge*

PRINTED IN GREAT BRITAIN
BY EBENEZER BAYLIS AND SON, LTD.
THE TRINITY PRESS, WORCESTER, AND LONDON

For
my friends
at the Savile Club

CONTENTS

FOREWORD

THESE essays and papers were all written during the years 1951–60. Some have been published; half a dozen, having formed the subjects of my private Christmas cards, are already familiar to only a few; two published articles ('Fowler' and 'Australian English') now appear in their manuscript, rather more comprehensive, versions; 'H. L. Mencken' was broadcast by the B.B.C., European Division; three ('Dictionaries', 'Clichés', 'Paranoiacs and Psycholepts') are entirely new; 'Some Aspects of Etymology' —read as a paper to a seminar—has not been published.

The essays range from the slight, all in Section I, to the rather more solid, especially in Section V. Two or three apparently etymological essays belong really to other sections and have been placed there. In any such loose division of subject and manner, a certain amount of overlapping is inevitable —and only the formalists will, or at any rate should, object.

ERIC PARTRIDGE

GENERAL

THE SHAGGY DOG[1]

A True Story

THE 'shaggy dog' story has developed from an idea recorded
in literature some 2,400 years ago. As you might expect, the
Greeks had a word for it—at least, for the idea: *para prosdokian*,
contrary to expectation. The most important feature of 'shaggy
dogs' is the unexpectedness of their endings, although that in
itself is not enough to make a story 'shaggy'.

The Roman comedy-writers carried on the idea, which
forms part of a tradition almost as old as the human race. But
to call it a tradition is to understate: the origin of this sort of
thing lies in that spirit of mischief which characterizes all such
human beings as take neither themselves nor others too
seriously. From this spirit of mischief have sprung the catch-
story, the epigram, and the tall story. In one sense the 'shaggy
dog' forms a special aspect of the catch-story; in another, of the
ordinary witty story, exemplified perhaps first in the very
ancient Greek example: A pert youth, meeting an old crone
driving a small herd, cried, Good morning, mother of asses!—
Good morning, my son.

The Greeks were masters of the epigram; the Romans took it
from them and, in their turn, passed it to the medieval European scholars. Among the inheritors were Britons. Alexander
Pope, another master of the epigram, caused to be engraved on
the collar of a dog he presented in 1736 to His Royal Highness,
this couplet:

> I am his Highness' dog at Kew;
> Pray tell me, Sir, whose dog are you?

[1] My *The 'Shaggy Dog' Story*—its origin, development and nature, with a
few seemly examples—appeared several months after this article was
published in *The Sydney Morning Herald*. The book was deliciously illustrated
with line-drawings by V. H. Drummond and remains in print.

Another factor in the gradual development of the 'shaggy dog' story was the catch-poem, as written by Oliver Goldsmith, Tom Hood and later practitioners. It was Goldsmith who sang of the mad dog that bit a man, a very touching poem with its mordant conclusion, 'The dog it was that died'. That poem has, with variations, passed into folklore and has even originated the journalistic advice, handed by every conscientious editor to every cub reporter: If a dog bites a man, it's a very ordinary occurrence; if a man bites a dog, it's news.

Passing to the latter half of the nineteenth century, we come to a good example of the folk-story, a funny story current the whole world over. I have heard the following story in Australia, New Zealand, England, Scotland; it is, I'm told, known in Canada and South Africa; and wherever it is told it has the proper local setting and is claimed as indigenous. After a long, tiring day, two drovers halted for the night. The simple meal having been eaten in silence by these two strong, silent men, one of them gazed into the starlit distance. 'Horse,' he remarked. Joining him, the other gazed even harder. 'Cow,' he said. The next morning, the first speaker packed his few things. 'Going somewhere?' asked the second. 'Yes; too much so-and-so talk around here.'

Other contributions to the evolution of the catch-story towards the 'shaggy dog' were provided by such diverse literary forms as the limerick:

> There was a young lady of Riga
> Who smiled as she rode on a tiger:
> They returned from the ride
> With the lady inside,
> And the smile on the face of the tiger;

as the clerihew, a verse-form invented by Edward Clerihew Bentley:

> What I like about Clive
> Is that he is no longer alive.
> There is a great deal to be said
> For being dead;

and as the tall story, not indeed invented by Americans but certainly perfected by them:

A farmer kept a cow and calf out at pasture. If he wanted them for anything, he rang a bell to call them home. One day he heard a loud noise in the farmyard. Hastening outside, he saw an unusual sight. A swarm of mosquitoes had eaten the cow—and were ringing the bell to call the calf.

A factor even more important was the peculiar twist imparted to catch-stories early in the present century, as in that of the two strangers on a train. One looked up from his newspaper and said, 'Very interesting article here. About ghosts.'—'All rubbish! I don't believe in that sort of nonsense.'—'*Don't* you?' said the other—and vanished.

Somewhere about 1906 arrived the earliest of all genuine 'shaggy dog' stories. During World War One it was put into uniform and told of a young officer on leave in Paris. It has since received yet other forms, but the essential feature is that a man picks up a letter he cannot read, gets into all sorts of trouble when others read it for him, and finally, just when he is about to solve the mystery, finds that he has lost the letter.

From January 31, 1924, the date of his first broadcast, until shortly before his death in 1941, A. J. Alan, whose real name was Leslie Harrison Lambert, entertained radio listeners with his seemingly artless stories, many of which had something in common with 'shaggy dogs' and one of which, 'The Diver' (broadcast on Christmas Day, 1925), contained the earliest 'shaggy dog' to achieve a vast audience and reputable print; it appeared in *Good Evening, Everyone!* 1928. 'A. J. Alan', a king among broadcasters, did more than anyone else to set the scene for the 'shaggy dog' as we know it today, and his own stories in this kind, embedded within his radio stories, did much to popularize the kind itself. Alan's 'shaggy dogs' had a tremendous influence, despite their fewness; I can remember only two—that of the disgruntled shark in 'The Diver' and that of Hilarion the Goldfish.

The next man to endow the 'shaggy dog' with literary merit was the distinguished American dramatist, novelist and essayist, Christopher Morley, who in *John Mistletoe*, 1931, told a delight-

ful story of 'a small hairy dog': a story that clearly has influenced the very name of this art-form.

Since those days, the 'shaggy dog' has attracted less of
literary, more of public attention. It has strengthened its
position in the United States and invaded the British
Dominions, where, by the way, the harrowing tale of the young
army officer and the mysterious letter had, since 1918 or 1919,
been heard from time to time. Its widespread currency and
popularity, attested by the fact that highbrows and exclusives
try to obtain a reputation for superiority of mind and taste by
affecting to despise it and, when they think they can get away
with a pose, by pretending to know none, have resulted in an
improvement of quality. A good 'shaggy dog' possesses a wittily
sudden and unexpected ending, all the more unexpected that
the 'lead-in' and the 'lead-up' have had to be leisurely, almost
diffuse, and deceptively factual and matter-of-fact; narrative
and dialogue mingle skilfully but unnoticeably; no matter how
absurd, a 'shaggy dog' must never be silly; and it is clean.

Asked for an example, one is at a disadvantage. So many
stories clamour for attention; some are too long; yet the longer
are usually—and very naturally—the better. The following
stories, though short, do not lack merit.

Travelling by train to London from one of its outer dormi-
tories, a businessman got into a compartment and was amazed
to see a middle-aged passenger playing chess with a handsome
Newfoundland. The players moved the pieces swiftly and
surely. Just before the train pulled in at the London terminus,
the game ended, with the dog victorious. 'That's an extra-
ordinary dog, beating you like that—and obviously you're
pretty good yourself.'—'Oh, I don't think he's so hot; I beat
him in the two games before that.'

Which reminds me of the American story about a dog carrying on a long and animated conversation with a parrot. It
happened in a saloon, and the bartender congratulated the
owner of these two gifted creatures. 'Aw, well, I think I ought
to tell you, the act's not on the level.'—'Not on the level! What
do you mean?'—'I mean, not on the level. You see, the dog is a
ventriloquist.'

Which resembles the story of that mouse which, standing on the counter in an American bar room, gaily sang 'Annie Laurie'. When another customer offered to buy the mouse, the owner exclaimed, 'You don't have to buy him. Buy me a drink and I'll *give* him to you.' The other man hastily did so, hastily pocketed the mouse, hastily departed. The bartender exclaimed, 'Why did you do a crazy thing like that? Parting with a gold mine!'—'Don't you believe it. "Annie Laurie" is the only song that mouse *can* sing.'

Which seems to be a suitable note on which to conclude.

SOURCES OF CONTAMINATION

In his poem *James Russell Lowell*, 1894, John Greenleaf Whittier the American poet declared that

> From purest wells of English undefiled
> None deeper drank than he, the New World's child.

As not every schoolboy knows, Whittier was deliberately alluding to a statement made almost exactly three centuries earlier: Edmund Spenser's

> Dan Chaucer, well of English undefiled.

Never undefiled in its sources—but then, no European language ever has been undefiled in its sources—English can be, and often has been, uncontaminated in style, despite the constant assault made upon it, both by all the usual enemies of a language, such as jargon, slang, dialect, foreign words, and by Americanisms. Before we glance at these sources of contamination, we must bear in mind the complementary truth that English has long been enriched by recruits from these very sources. The apparent contradiction is no contradiction at all: the war between good and evil takes place no less constantly in language than in the spiritual, moral and political spheres.

It does not fall to me to discuss such enemies of linguistic purity as slovenly writing and woolly thinking; they form a quite different though admittedly cognate subject. Of the relevant sources of contamination, jargon is one of the most prolific of impurity. Jargon has been defined as 'the technical, esoteric, or secret vocabulary of a science, art, trade, sect, profession, or other special group' (Webster).

These special vocabularies are excusable and often unavoidable in their proper place; they become objectionable when they invade the general vocabulary and displace better words. The *emanate, transpire, eventuate* of journalese are bad enough in journalism, but, adopted by self-respecting writers and by other educated persons, they shock and repel. The *advise* (tell), *favour* (letter), *esteemed order, substantial percentage* (much), *under one's signature* and *your good selves* (you) of commercialese may pass unnoticed in the secretarial secrecies of commerce, but they strike one as ludicrous when they are used outside. The *animal feeding stuffs* (fodder), *communicate* (tell, inform), *through the usual channels* (normally; in the usual way), *at a high(er)*, or *at the highest, level, endeavour, it would seem that* (apparently) of officialese do not—would that they did!—cause a riot in Whitehall or Washington or Canberra, but elsewhere they are intolerably pompous and excruciatingly wordy.

The jargon of science is less painful; it should, however, be confined to scientific contexts. More dangerous is the jargon of psychology, especially of psychiatry—that branch of medicine combined with psychology which deals with mental disorders and moral aberrations. Look at the way in which *inferiority complex* is misused and *complex* itself misunderstood! Otherwise reputable persons may be heard asking 'What is your *reaction* to—or, How do you *react* to—this or that?' When all they mean is, 'What do you think of, or about, it? What is your opinion?' People who should know better are forever confusing *psychoses* with *neuroses*, and using either or both of them where an ordinary English word would be infinitely preferable. As for *sublimation* and *subliminal, lesion* and *trauma*. . . . !

More important, perhaps, is the contamination that results from an unwise substitution of dialect, slang, and foreign terms for Standard English words. The use of such terms is forgivable in dialogue, where they help to maintain an air of naturalness— if the speakers use these terms—and do not reflect adversely upon the ability of the author to write good English. But a writer betrays himself when, instead of a good English word, he elsewhere uses one from dialect or slang or a foreign language. There was a period when it was thought smart and fashionable and, in short, meritorious to borrow from French, and many novelists and short-story writers sprinkled their pages with gallicisms. The fault is now much less common. Even 'a *je ne sais quoi*' for an indefinable something is on the way out. That darling of literary critics, *rebarbative* (French *rébarbatif*), surly of

humour or crabbed of style, has had a very short life; as
Stephen Potter has remarked in his scintillating *One-Upness*, it
is no longer 'an O.K. word'. But *décor* has probably come to
stay: yet in what except brevity is it superior to 'decoration' or
'setting'? Slang and dialect are likewise used less than they
were, except, of course, in dialogue.

Closely allied to the sources already mentioned is that increasingly potent influence, Americanization, which operates
at all grades or levels: not only dialect and slang, not only
official and scientific jargon, but also the ordinary good
American English—that is, Standard American. (Professor
W. Cabell Greet, of Columbia University, New York, has
shown that, as there is a Standard English, so there is a Standard American: and it's time that this self-evident fact became
evident to all those who should have been the first to recognize
it. As Britons should use the one, so Americans should use the
other.)

For instance, why abandon excellent British English, i.e.
Standard English, for American Standard English, excellent
though it be in the United States? Yet this is precisely what
happens when an English, a Scottish, an Australian writer (or
speaker) indulges himself in this sort of thing:

'The whole caboodle (or, set-up) is phoney'—the whole thing
is suspect.

'That guy never faces up to the facts'—that fellow never faces
the facts.

'The bellhop will take you to the elevator'—the bellboy will
take you to the lift.

'This editorial is a swell piece of writing'—this leader (or,
leading article) is very well written.

Americanisms, foreign words, terms from slang and dialect,
official and scientific and other jargon, all can be included in
the condemnatory verdict:

a deliberate or, at best, unthinking use of unnecessary words.

BUSINESS ENGLISH
AND ITS CONFEDERATES

Not all business English is bad. Far from it. I know a publisher, an editor, a business man, all of whom write admirable business letters: concise, lucid, pertinent, yet neither so detached as to be cold nor so dispassionate as to be forbidding. Business English is gradually improving; the standard is far higher now than even thirty years ago. The same applies to what I have called 'its confederates'—journalese on one side, officialese on the other.

This improvement in all three branches is due to two main factors. These are the general movement of all writing, whether literary or journalistic, official or commercial, the letters of the educated or those of the semi-educated, away from the pompous and the ponderous, the elegant and the genteel, a movement in accord with the changing tempo of civilization; and the particular advice of certain public benefactors. Of these benefactors the most influential have perhaps been Sir Arthur Quiller-Couch, who in 1913 at Cambridge delivered a witty lecture on 'Jargon', reprinted in 1916, and still available, in *On the Art of Writing*: the late and much lamented H. W. Fowler, in *A Dictionary of Modern English Usage*, 1926: A.P., now Sir Alan, Herbert, in *What a Word!* published in the middle 1930's and often reprinted: Sir Ernest Gowers in *Plain Words*, 1948, and in *The A.B.C.* of the same subject, 1951: myself, in *Usage and Abusage*, 1947, and *British and American English since 1900* (in collaboration with John W. Clark), 1951.

Sir Arthur Quiller-Couch attacked officialese, journalese and commercialese, as also did H. W. Fowler. Sir Alan Herbert concentrated upon commercialese, with side-glances at the other two enemies. Sir Ernest Gowers, addressing his fellow Civil Servants, naturally deals, in the main, with officialese. I have treated of all three vices.

21

But, before considering these three forms of wrongdoing, let us settle the question of nomenclature.

Commercialese, a term formed, like officialese, on the analogy of journalese, has also been called officese, to be avoided because of its similarity to officialese. Commercialese is likewise called business English. Strictly, business English should mean the English used in the transaction of business, but in practice it is mostly regarded as synonymous with commercialese, which is the worst kind of English used in business.

Journalese, itself perhaps on the analogy of Johnsonese (the style of Dr Samuel Johnson when writing in his more ponderous manner), is journalistic English of the worse kind; obviously much journalistic writing is good, some of it very good indeed—good, that is, for its purpose. All writing, whether prose or verse, is to be judged by its suitability to the purpose. A lyric poet does not write like a business man, nor a business man like a poet. A style eminently suitable for one subject may be not merely unsuitable but ludicrous for another. One does not expect an official letter to be written with the wit and charm of a letter by Cowper or Lamb, Wilde or Meredith, Walter Raleigh (the scholar) or George Gordon. The historical style of Gibbon or Macaulay, Froude or Trevelyan, transcends the needs of a reporter describing a street accident.

Officialese is often called official jargon or simply jargon; simply yet confusingly, for both journalese and commercialese are equally jargon. In America they call it either Federal prose, humorously Washington Choctaw, that weighty sort of official English which is issued from Washington, and which corresponds to Whitehallese, or gobbledygook, the language of lesser officials and of politicians. Then there is that shocking abortion of English which is perpetrated by official economists: economese.

To generalize about officialese, journalese, commercialese is almost fatally easy. I could write this article without once touching earth. 'Example is better than precept.' Let us look at a few brief examples of each kind of writing before we examine business English in some detail.

When a journalist or an official speaks of *information emanating and transpiring at the highest level* he is using both journalese (*emanating and transpiring*) and officialese (*at the highest level*). He is also very conveniently illustrating a *significant*, or important, and *sinister*, or dangerous tendency : the tendency of journalese to infect the language of officials, and that of officialese to impress journalists. When an official uses *ult.*, *inst.*, *prox.*, he has been contaminated by commercialese. If a business man speaks of *incidents* when he means quarrels, he has been influenced by journalism, and if he says that a certain matter can be decided only *at a higher level* he too has borrowed from the vocabulary of officialdom.

All three classes of person—the official, the journalist, the business man—tend to be influenced by the other two, which-ever the other two happen to be. If they all wrote Standard English they would run no such risk. But then, if they all wrote Standard English, there would exist, there could exist, no such things as officialese, journalese, commercialese. This inter-influence is unavoidable. The most we can, in an imperfect world, ask, because the most we can expect, is that the terms proper to officials be left to officials; that journalists should use no more officialese and journalese than their duties oblige them to use; and that business men should ape neither officials nor journalists. Heaven knows, every one of these three classes of person has quite enough to do to keep its own house clean !

Journalese may be exemplified by a quotation that I have used elsewhere. It occurred a little over a century ago, yet it could easily have been written today and will probably be written tomorrow.

'Notwithstanding the genuine literary productions that have sprung out of'—at least not, we thankfully notice, *emanated from* —'the haunts of cotton mills and weaving sheds, they have only here and there penetrated far beyond the immediate neighbour-hood that called them into existence' (a Manchester journalist, 1850). Put into ordinary English, the sentence might read :— 'Despite the literature that has come from the industrial areas, it has seldom been noticed outside them.'

Officialese we have, every adult of us, encountered at some time or other, especially in the fascinating pages of *How to Fill up Your Form*, the engaging leaflet sent to all those who are so fortunate as to pay income tax: after all, the one thing worse than paying it is *not* having any to pay. This annual bringer of glad tidings has improved both its manners and its English; the same improvement has, I'm told, been remarked in the United States about the corresponding form. But *How to Fill up Your Form* could be further improved. For instance, 'How Profits Are to Be Calculated' is inferior to 'How to Reckon Profits'. Among the 'Expenses which cannot be allowed include' (why not 'Taxable expenses include'?) we find 'Cost of maintaining yourself or your family or payments for any other domestic or private purposes', which might perhaps be rewritten 'Your or your family's living expenses and amusements'. 'No deduction can ordinarily be claimed for the cost of travelling between your residence and your place of employment' might advantageously be changed to 'You cannot claim allowances for the cost of travelling to and from work'. Without being pernickety or hypercritical, a good writer—in short, a clear thinker—could simplify the form and reduce its 'wordage' by at least one-fifth.

Thus, by easy transition, we arrive at commercialese. To list the monstrosities permitted—nay, encouraged—by many business men would be out of place in an essay or even an article. Instead, I shall give an example of the sort of thing still far too common.

'Dear Sir,

We are in receipt of your esteemed favour of the 31st ult. with regard to the estimate you require for the packing and removal of your books and other personal effects from your residence at 17 The Willows, Arcana, to your prospective residence at 19 The Oaks, Refuge, on the 20th inst. We take great pleasure in asking you to confirm an arrangement whereby our representative would call on you, on the 4th inst. at 3 p.m., in order to make an inspection of the above mentioned books and effects preliminary to calculating the number of cases we shall need to effect the packing and subsequent removal of same. We trust that the suggested time will suit your convenience and that we may then be entrusted

with the required estimate and enjoy the favour of undertaking this work for you. We shall then issue our quotation
and hope to receive an early reply from your good self. The
time you suggest for the removal, 8.30 a.m., would be entirely convenient.

Assuring you of our best attention at all times,
We beg to remain,
Yours faithfully,
Burble & Burble, Ltd.'

That letter could have been written more briefly and pleas-
ingly in several ways. The following amendment should be
taken, not as the best, but merely as preferable to the removers'
letter.

'Dear Sir,
Thank you for your letter of May 31. Shall our man call, at
3 p.m., June 4, to estimate the cost? If the quotation suits,
our van will call at 8.30 a.m., June 20.
Yours faithfully,
Burble & Burble, Ltd.'

The trouble with much business English is that it is so very
inefficient: excessively and exasperatingly wordy; addicted to
un-English activities; using an outmoded jargon; unnecessarily
obsequious. Be polite, yes! Politeness oils the wheels of trade
and commerce. But not grateful for something that may never
happen.

To write as these removers did is to waste time and paper, to
obscure the salient needs and facts, and to insult the English
language, which can be as brief, polished, clear as any other
language, French included. Such a letter seems to imply that
the writer thinks the other fellow a blithering idiot. For instance, the inquiry must have been received; an estimate has
to be made; only if the inquirer approves the estimate and
therefore, in effect, confirms the removal, will the van call for
the goods.

It is easy, far too easy, to write a letter in which occur all the
well-worn terms, all the long-winded phrases, all the substitutes

for thinking. Only rarely is it possible, for the circumstances usually need to be detailed, to achieve the brevity that a business acquaintance and I, fired by his example, once achieved. I had overlooked an account long overdue. He sent a dated statement and the accompanying note:

> 'Dear Mr Partridge,
> Please!
> _____,'

By return of post I sent a cheque, with a note:

> 'Dear Mr ——,
> Herewith.
> E— P—'

By return, he wrote:

> 'Dear Mr Partridge,
> Thanks!
> _____,'

That exchange of notes was, I maintain, business-like; my note admittedly a shade less courteous than his. At the time, he was at the head, as he still is, of a very large business.

Translated into commercialese, the correspondence would have gone something like this:

> 'Dear Sir,
> The enclosed statement will show that this debt was incurred almost three years ago. If it is not paid immediately, we shall be forced to take action.
> Yours faithfully,
> Managing Director.'

> 'Dear Sir,
> I regret exceedingly that this oversight should have occurred. Herewith please find enclosed my cheque for the amount involved.
> Yours faithfully,
> _____,'

Some days later, the cheque having been cleared at the bank:

'Dear Sir,

Your favour of the —th received. Please find our receipt enclosed herewith.

Now that the matter has been satisfactorily settled, we should be glad to do business with you again.

We are, Sir,

Yours faithfully,

_____,

A fitting reply to that letter would be—. But no, perhaps not.

It is so much easier to use all the well-known conventional phrases and stopgaps—*the matter is receiving our best attention, in due course, with the minimum of delay*, etc.—than to think; so much easier to pad than to prune; so much easier to gorge than to diet. Almost before one realizes it, a letter has got itself written: but that is no way to write a letter of any kind whatsoever. On a busy day, one perhaps shrinks from the effort needed to write one clear, helpful, strictly relevant, comprehensive letter after another. With a little practice, however, one finds that the pleasure derived from writing well lessens the fatigue. Soon, too, the fatigue decreases; soon, indeed, there will be no fatigue.

Admittedly one can hardly be expected to correct faults if one does not know what they are. The chief faults in bad business English are these: 'Passing the buck'—whether directly or indirectly. Blaming general conditions instead of admitting faulty organization within the firm as a whole or one's own particular mistake. This cowardice shows itself also in using such indirect expressions as *it would seem that*, owing to an oversight, a mistake was perhaps made. If the writer of a letter is responsible, let him take the responsibility: ultimately, someone has to take it. Business men are not expected to be supermen. Honesty and sincerity will usually outweigh an error.

Allied to such cowardice is the preference of the passive—*it is believed that*, for *I believe that*—to the active. This tendency often goes so far that a writer uses two or even three passives in one sentence. For instance: '*It is thought* by the management that the work *could not possibly be carried out* in the time *stipulated by you*', instead of 'We think that we could not complete the work in the time you stipulate'.

The preference of long words to short. 'We do not *contemplate* the *possibility* of such an *eventuality*', for 'We do not think that such a thing will happen' or, better, '. . . that this will happen'. *After prolonged consideration* rarely means more than *after much thought*.

The preference of long sentences to short. 'When you have given the matter the attention which we feel it deserves—and we urge you to consider it very carefully indeed, for its importance can hardly be exaggerated—we shall, if you wish to pursue the matter further, be happy to afford you all the assistance within our power' could take the form: 'Please consider the matter carefully. Then, if you wish to go ahead, we shall help as best we can.'

Abstract or, at the best, very vague instead of concrete words and phrases. '*National circumstances* are such as to *necessitate* a comprehensive *alteration* of financial policy and a consequent *reduction* of *capital expenditure* in both the *domestic* and the *foreign market*'—'Events force us to spend less both at home and abroad'.

And perhaps the worst and most frequent of all faults: the tendency to think that one's correspondent has no memory, doesn't know what he is doing, needs to have every 'i' double-dotted and every 't' double-crossed, and is, in short, a fool.

The remedy is easy. Write as if you believe your correspondent to be intelligent; write as compactly, briefly, simply and directly as you can; keep closely to the point; write as if you are not only responsible for what you write but also responsible for what you do; be polite and pleasant.

THE ETYMOLOGY OF ADVERTISING

The technical vocabulary—the specialized language—of advertising is, compared with that of (say) painting or the theatre, rather small. It is, however, large enough to demand a fair-sized monograph. To perform this *multum in parvo* of compression, I must restrict myself to a very few terms; and, even at that, deal with only their etymologies or word-histories. Now, this is a pity, for, of all the arts, advertising has the most decidedly come-hither eye and the most provocative ways.

To the general public, *advertising* and *publicity* differ, in that the former is a part of the latter; to the dyed-in-the-wool, whole-hogger, one-hundred-per-center of an advertising man and woman, they tend to be synonymous, or, rather, publicity is merely a part of advertising, or so they tell me. *Advertising* depends only partly upon *advertisements*. Both words obviously derive from 'to *advertise*', from the French *advertir*, to call attention to, from L *advertere*, short for *advertere mentem*, to turn (*vertere*) the mind (*mens*) to or towards (*ad*) something. The entire art of commercial advertising consists in precisely that: turning the public's mind towards certain goods.

Publicity is both passive, the state of being known or of being made known to the public, and active, the art and practice of making known to the public a person, cause, thing; the specialist in this art and practice is a *publicity agent* or simply a *publicity man* (compare *advertising man*); a *publicist* is a journalist or writer specializing in causes. The word *publicity* has been adapted from French *publicité*, itself from *public*, available to all, a word that, like its derivative noun, was promptly adopted by English. The French adjective *public* comes from Latin *publicus*, an altered contraction of *populicus*, belonging to the *populus* or people in general. Both *advertise* (and *advertisement*) and *publicity* have been borrowed from France. Nor are they strange in this respect.

Campaign, as in 'an advertising *campaign*', refers to a well-planned, long-lasting, extensive series of advertisements and newspaper paragraphs and even society notes and, in the United States, a series of programmes on radio and television, such as that for Beautee Soap wittily and satirically described in *The Hucksters*, a novel by Frederic Wakeman, who derisively and violently blows the lid off the American radio-publicity racket. The French *campaigne* or *campagne*, country suitable for military movements, hence the movements of the *armée en campagne* (army in the field) over a period, comes from Italian *campagna*, from Latin *campania*, a plain (compare the It *Campagna*, L *Campania*), itself an extension of *campus*, a field, whence, incidentally, our *camp*, from an army's tents being pitched in a *campus*.

Often used in advertising are cartoons: and *cartoon* owes something both to F *carton* and to its source, the It. *cartone*, a large *carta* or drawing, from Late L *carta*, *charta*, a mostly stiff piece of paper, from L *charta*, leaf of paper, from Gr *khartēs*, leaf of paper, originally a layer of papyrus, 'paper' being here used very loosely. (*Paper*, just in case you've forgotten the fact, comes, through Old French, from L *papyrus*, a transliteration of Gr *papuros*.) Odd how frequently, indeed predominantly, Frenchmen and ancient Greeks pop up in the history of civilization; yet how appositely, for advertising is a highly civilized art, however barbarous its opponents think it.

But the remaining terms I shall mention are not of French origin. *Glossy*, for a fashionable illustrated magazine printed on shiny 'art' paper, comes from the United States of America. Properly it is the adjective of *gloss*, the lustre of a smooth, polished surface, and *gloss* apparently derives from Old Norse *glossi*, a blaze, a glow, from *gloa*, the source of our *glow*: a shiny surface glows.

Solus, literally 'a single', whether in space or in time, is obviously the Latin adjective *solus*, alone, as in its English derivative *sole*, or lonely, as in *solitary*, from L *solitarius* (whence also the F *solitaire*, the game of patience, played by one person), an extension of *solus*.

Usually alone on a page, but always gazing boldly upon the world of genuine readers and moronic lookers, is that advertising technicality the *window*, a picturesque term—and almost the only one that, in the entire vocabulary of publicity, could fairly be called poetic. Advertising has the perhaps unmerited reputation of rapidly drying the ocular moisture of dewy-eyed beginners; the artillerymen of advertising remain realistically clear-eyed as they aim at the sentimental heart of the buying public. Ah, yes! *window*. . . . *Windoge* in Middle English, it represents the Old Norse *vindauga*, window, literally the *auga* or eye of the *vindr* or wind. As a poetic compound, *window* ranks with *daisy*, for the ME *daies ie*, earlier *daies eige*, derives from Old English *daeges eage*, day's eye, in reference to that yellow disc which, at the flower's centre, resembles a tiny sun.

My other choices, though earthy, have an Anglo-Saxon forthrightness. The plan or *make-up* of an advertisement is a *lay-out*; it is so laid out as best to catch the wandering eye. A lay-out is perhaps seen most advantageously in the *poster*, a device that has enormously progressed since 1920. This *poster* was probably suggested by *bill-poster*, where *poster* means nothing more than 'placer'. On the other hand, a full-page advertisement, whether illustrated or not, is usually called either a *splash* or, if showy, a *splurge*; both words evoke the idea of *display*, the former being prompted by 'to *make a splash*' and the latter blending into an echoic amalgam the two words *spl*ash and *urge*. Beside them the much older, equally echoic *puff* seems weak and trivial.

Whether tiny puff or gorgeous splurge or magnificent poster, an advertisement has often passed through a period of elephantine gestation. All *copy writers* or, in radio advertising, *script writers*, have soon learnt to grin or, at any rate, to bear it when their first or second or later attempts have been rejected. The generation now in its sixties has used at least three terms for 'to reject' or, more drastically, 'to cancel' : *dish*, probably from 'to *dis*card' ; *can*, an Americanism, perhaps from 'to put into the trash can' ; *kill*, another Americanism, as in the punning title of Bagby's 'thriller', *Red Is for Killing*.

WHEN IS BAD GRAMMAR GOOD?

BAD grammar is never good.

But what one generation holds to be bad grammar is occasionally adjudged by the next generation to be good: and the new generation loses no time in wondering why on earth the formerly condemned practice was ever condemned at all. Nor is the feeling confined to young and vigorous countries such as Australia or the United States, New Zealand and South Africa. Oddly enough, it is usually the young countries which cling longest to certain grammatical conventions, partly for the same reason that causes them to cling to and retain words that, in Britain, have long passed into disuse. This retention, however, has occurred more frequently in the United States than in the British Dominions.

There are two quite remarkable instances of bad grammar becoming good. When I was at school, or might have been, in the first decade of this century, I should have been reprimanded —if not worse—if I had ended a sentence with a preposition. As one of my reprimanders said, all unconscious of the irony, '*With* is a bad word to end a sentence *with*'. In *The King's English*, 1906, the brothers Fowler of sainted memory spoke of 'the modern superstition against putting a preposition at the end' and most appositely cited the Authorized Version's 'I will not leave thee, until I have done that which I have spoken to thee of'. When, twenty years later, the surviving brother H. W. Fowler's classic, *A Dictionary of Modern English Usage*, appeared, the brothers' campaign had succeeded.

The other remarkable instance is that of the former prejudice against splitting an infinitive: you could split your opponent's skull and merely incur a hanging and all was over; but no editor dared to split even an enemy's infinitive and would have committed suicide if he had found himself doing so, the obloquy would have been too terrible, the scorn implacable.

Nowadays the veriest mouse of a man can split an infinitive and do it light-heartedly and, what is so much better, unthinkingly. Where formerly we felt bound to write 'It is necessary immediately to arrange a meeting' or 'to arrange immediately a meeting' we now write either 'It is necessary to immediately arrange a meeting' or, if we have any sense, 'It is necessary to arrange a meeting immediately', which, despite what a few purblind pundits assert, is the usual English order or, to phrase it philologically, 'accords with syntactical usage'. It is, however, to be noted that whereas, theorctically, we may safely split any infinitive whatsoever, in practice there are many we don't split, for reasons of euphony or style or even convenience.

Usage has decided to approve of final prepositions and split infinitives. Usage has been right to so decide. (Stylistically 'Usage has been right, so to decide' is preferable.) It is easy to be wise after the event: it's almost impossible to be wise before a linguistic event. Nevertheless, I shall 'stick my neck out' and particularize five potential changes that will, I think, become usage.

First, *whom* will probably disappear, to leave *who* the sole form apart from *whose*. Such constructions as '*Who* were you with last night?'—'*Who*'s that present for?'—'You'll support—*who*?'—'In the riot, it didn't seem to matter who hit *who*'—'I'll see *who* I like, when I like and why I like'—are already very common. Nor is it difficult to understand why, if you examine such sentences as '*Who* did you declare was at the party?' and '*Whom* do you declare to have been at the party'; or as 'As to *who* it was, I couldn't say'. Doubtless it will take longer for such contexts as 'For *who* is it?'—'Against *who* are you playing?'—'John, against *who* I was playing'—to become usage; and perhaps they never will, for usage can be extraordinarily arbitrary. But the '*Who* did you see when you went to Sydney?' type of sentence will most probably become general: compare the French '*Qui* as-tu vu, chérie?' (*Who*'d you see, sweet?); yet the French are a devastatingly logical people.

Secondly, *like* will probably supersede *as*, or at the least be used indifferently for it, in such sentences as 'He was ill, *like* I

2

told you, Ma'. The conjunction *for* began as *for that* (on account of that, because)—where, obviously, *for* was a preposition. Historically, linguistically, sensibly, *like* for 'as' is unexceptionable: by 99 per cent of Americans, it has already been accepted.

Purists (I among them) still object to *between* as an exact synonym of *among*. Nobody says '*among* two persons'; but many say '*between* three, or five, or fifty persons', where the purist— rightly, I think—says '*Among* three, or five, or fifty persons'. Whereas *among* will presumably, though far from certainly, continue to be restricted to more than two, *between* will probably come to be used for all numbers over one. Very similar is the puristic objection to *each other* being used of more than two and to *one another* of less than three persons or things. I write 'He and she loved *each other*' and 'Those three, or five, or fifty men will kill *one another* if they're not careful with that bomb'; but there is an increasing tendency among the majority of people to write indifferently 'He and she loved *each other*' or 'He and she loved *one another*'—'Those three, or five, or fifty men will kill *one another*'—or '*each other*'—'if they're not careful'. Although I myself preserve the distinction, I recognize that it is, in the main, artificial.

Then there's 'between you and *I*' or 'He actively dislikes Bill, Harry, Mary and *I*'. Yet the person saying those two things would not, unless he were illiterate, say 'For *I*', nor yet 'He dislikes *I*': one reason is that the pronoun does not, in the former instances, come immediately after the verb or the preposition governing it, the need for the accusative or objective case being consequently forgotten. But another reason, probably the predominant reason, is that 'You and *I*' and 'Bill, Harry, Mary and *I*' are apprehended as units or, at worst, as physical pluralities serving as psychological units.

There are a few other instances where usage will probably change. *Will* and *would* will, I think, oust *shall* and *should*; in America, they have largely done so already; in Australia, I hear, they are fast doing so. The disappearance of *shall* and *should* will simplify speech and writing: it would also destroy two valuable sets of distinctions.

Usage is as usage does, and nobody can do anything very much about it, except now and then help it on its way.

(Written on September 17, 1952. Published in *The Sydney Morning Herald,* 1952.)

PUNCTUATION—FRIEND,
NOT ENEMY

How often do we hear the following or uncomfortably similar remarks, very often from those who are unable to punctuate anything more solid than a paper bag! 'Punctuation is a necessary evil; necessary, yet an evil'—'No good writer depends on his stops'—'Good punctuation doesn't mean good writing'— 'Only the fussy and the pernickety worry about punctuation'— 'Look after your writing and your punctuation will look after itself'—'You need only two stops, the full stop and the comma, so why bother with semicolons and colons?'—'Punctuation is for pedants'.

Of all those remarks, only one merits a second thought: 'Look after your writing and your punctuation will look after itself': for the very simple reason that good writing includes good punctuation.

To regard punctuation as an evil, is to exaggerate; to regard it as a nuisance, is merely to admit to laziness; to regard it as an enemy, is to convict oneself of muddled thinking, for it is an ally. But it is something more than an ally; it is far more positive and helpful than a mere ally: it is a friend.

First, however, we in our turn must take care not to exaggerate. Punctuation does not supersede a clear style; it forms an aid to a clear style. The stops are not devices that convert the bad into good; they serve to make the good still better. Punctuation does not create; it assists. On the other hand, punctuation does not form an ornament of style; it forms a part of style. So far from being haphazard and perfunctory, punctuation is—or should be—consistent and thorough and is, therefore, a skilled craft. Good punctuation is more than a craft; it is an art, for it demands variety and subtlety. As practised by a master, punctuation has grace.

This, however, is not an occasion I can use to expatiate upon the aesthetic and intellectual charms of The Higher Punctuation

—a subject that, along with the more pedestrian aspects, I treat in a book: *You Have a Point There*, subtitled A Practical Guide to Punctuation and Its Allies and Accessories.

Rather shall I show the usefulness and indeed the necessity of punctuation by exemplifying what happens when the punctuation is faulty either in quantity or in quality. (I say 'faulty', not 'defective', because too much punctuation is nearly as bad as—some declare that it is worse than—too little.) Nor shall I speak of rules and principles: here, more than in most subjects, theory without examples is horribly misleading or, at the least, irritatingly vague; here, more than in most subjects, examples imply, usually very closely imply, the few rules and the many principles.

So long ago as 1644, a Southwark schoolmaster named Richard Hodges wrote a little book, *The English Primrose*, and to give point to his advice on punctuation he quoted this badly stopped sentence:

'My Son, if sinners intise [entice] thee consent thou, not refraining thy foot from their way'—
instead of

'My Son, if sinners intise thee consent thou not, refraining thy foot from their way'.

A twentieth-century writer would insert a comma after 'thee', to indicate the pause.

A modern example is afforded by the letter of invitation despatched to Dr Jameson at the time of his raid into the Transvaal (1895). In the form cabled to *The Times* it reads:

'It is under these circumstances that we feel constrained to call upon you to come to our aid should a disturbance arise here the circumstances are so extreme that we cannot but believe that you and the men under you will not fail to come to the rescue of people who are so situated'.

The Times put a full stop after 'aid' and thus caused Jameson's impulsive act to appear to be justified, for the message then means 'Come immediately'. It is, however, believed that the writers of the letter intended the invitation to be conditional upon a circumstance arising in a very indefinite future and perhaps not at all: in short, that the full stop should have fallen not after 'aid' but after 'here'.

That was a very serious mistake, yet of a sort only too frequent. Compare a few sentences containing a punctuation less disastrous—but hardly less absurd and hardly less easily avoidable—and then, if you can, persist in decrying the importance of good punctuation; if, that is, you do decry it. Sometimes the only damage is a momentary bewilderment; but a serious and able writer does not wish to bewilder his readers.

'The question we know by now is meaningless'—probably the author means that 'the question, we know by now, is meaningless', so why doesn't he say so?

'And once I had discovered that there was no longer any doubt as to whether a spark of life still lingered in him'—at first one reads it as it has been written, as every reader is entitled to do, and only on reaching the full stop placed after 'him' does one realize that the sentence should have carried a comma after 'that'.

'You know John and Jill and Tom should know the three of you'—a woolly and distressingly ambiguous statement, for having survived the shock of finding that the writer doesn't mean what one was beginning to think he meant, one still does not know—in fact, one cannot know—whether he means:

'You know John and Jill, and Tom should know the three of you', where 'the three of you' signifies 'you, John, Jill'; or

'You know John, and Jill and Tom should know the three of you', where 'the three of you' could mean 'you, John, a third person—unnamed, but perhaps indicated'.

Now, if you happen to think that such mistakes are rare, I can only say, 'On the contrary, they are alarmingly frequent'. If you fondly suppose that *you* could not make mistakes either so silly or so obvious, I can only congratulate you upon your superiority to numerous distinguished authors and to myriads of very able men and women who, although not authors, do have to write letters, whether public or private, and perhaps also reports and memoranda, sometimes rather important ones.

Many a person has got into trouble because he was either so

lazy or so careless that he didn't take the trouble to punctuate correctly. As the late Dr Temple, Archbishop of York, wrote to *The Observer* (London) in October, 1938: 'If you are getting your commas, semicolons, and full stops wrong, it means that you are not getting your thoughts right, and your mind is muddled'.

DICTIONARIES

DICTIONARY is by far the commonest name for that means of communication between mind and mind, people and people, by which the meanings of words and phrases (arranged in strict alphabetical order) either in another or within one—usually one's own—language are ascertainable. In a one-way dictionary, the explanations are made in the same language as that of the words defined; in a two-way dictionary, the definitions are written in a language other than that of the words defined. *Dictionary* comes from Medieval Latin *dictionarium*, originally the neuter of *dictionarius*, itself elliptical for *dictionarius liber*, literally 'a word-book', from Latin *dictio*, a word (from *dicere*, to say)+-*arium*, -*arius*, the neuter and the masculine of a suffix that connotes 'a container of, a receptacle for' (whatever the core of the entire word may be).

'Word-book' supplies the key. Theoretically a dictionary can treat either of words or of things; but as the names of things, persons, places are themselves words, we nowadays tend to think of a *dictionary* as a book dealing with words and names—as being, in short, a word-book; a work that deals with subjects is properly called an *encyclopaedia*. An oblique yet quite invaluable sidelight on the social, educational and historical importance of the dictionary is shed by the number of names that have been applied to the various kinds of dictionary:

lexicon (from Greek *lexikon*, a dictionary, from *lexis*, a word), synonymous with *dictionary* in its predominant sense, but in modern practice applied mostly to an ancient language—for instance, Hebrew, Greek, Latin—as in Liddell and Scott's famous work, *A Greek-English Lexicon*;

glossary (Latin *glossarium*, from *glossa*, a difficult word, from Greek *glōssa*, the tongue), a dictionary of words either unusual (not forming part of the standard—e.g., not Standard English) or sectional (e.g., of a region or of a profession or trade) or period (of, e.g., the sixteenth century) or individual (the

language of Homer or Virgil, of Chaucer or Milton), this last
being sometimes called a *special dictionary*, with C. T. Onions's
A Shakespeare Glossary an outstanding example;

vocabulary (from Medieval Latin *vocabulum*, L *uocabulum*,
a name), a dictionary—usually with entries brief and terse—of
words, often only of the rare or difficult words, occurring
either in an old text (e.g., of Middle English) or in any foreign
work, especially if set as a text-book;

etymological dictionary, one in which the derivation and the
history of words form either the sole or the main feature, as in
Ernest Weekley's *A Concise Etymological Dictionary of Modern
English*;

concordance (literally, agreement), not strictly a dictionary at
all, but a mere alphabetical list—with all the relevant passages
—of all the words in a specific work (notably the Bible) or in a
specific author (especially Shakespeare); compare:

thesaurus (from Greek *thēsauros*, a store or hoard of things),
a dictionary or lexicon of all the words and all the phrases
in a language—obviously something that is possible only for a
language that is 'dead', the best example being the *Thesaurus
Linguae Latinae*.

It is important to remember those differences, even though
they tend to become mere distinctions, as when a *glossary* of
dialect, becoming very large, becomes a dictionary, as in the
best-known of all such works, Joseph Wright's immense and
invaluable storehouse, *The English Dialect Dictionary*.

Considering that dictionaries, apprehended in the wider,
the predominant acceptation, are so very important, indeed
indispensable, we learn with surprise that glossaries, in the
usual modern sense, long preceded them and were, in fact, the
earliest dictionaries. Neither the Romans nor the immensely
inquisitive Ancient Greeks wrote a dictionary of their own
language or of any foreign language: the Greeks did not, for
example, feel the need—or if they felt, they ignored the need—
of a dictionary of Egyptian, yet Greeks traded with, visited and
resided in Egypt, especially Alexandria, from an early period;
still more astonishingly, the Romans and other Italians had no
dictionary of Greek, yet Greek culture held in Imperial Rome

a position similar to that of French culture in the England of the Restoration and of the eighteenth century—and later. But we do know that in the seventh century B.C. there existed an Akkadian-Sumerian word-list, admittedly insignificant and inadequate, yet, by its very date, important. Glossaries of an author or of little-known words and phrases came quite early, the first of all being 'A Homer Glossary' (*Lexeis Homērikai*), written by the grammarian Apollonius the Sophist in the first century A.D. Many subsequent glossaries have disappeared; but Hesychius (fifth century, A.D.) continued their tradition and probably incorporated much of their work in his lexicon of Greek, notable for its recordings of dialectal forms and of rare words. A true dictionary of Greek did not appear until the sixteenth century: Henri Estienne's *Thesaurus Graecae Linguae* (1572). Oddly enough, it was his father Robert who, in his *Thesaurus Linguae Latinae* (1531), had laid the foundations of the Latin dictionary as we know it. The Estiennes were, of course, French; and to the French we owe many brilliant later examples of lexicography.

The modern languages possessed no adequate dictionaries until the late sixteenth century, although we may mention the *Promptorium Parvulorum*, in which a Dominican, Galfridus Grammaticus, had explained a number of English words—but in Latin. Of sixteenth to eighteenth century landmarks in the lexicography of the modern languages, one cannot omit the following, whether the English works: John Florio, *A World of Words, or most copious and exact dictionary in Italian and English*, 1598; Randle Cotgrave, *A Dictionary of the French and English Languages*, 1611; Henry Hexham, *A Copious English and Netherdutch Dictionary* (2 parts), 1648–58; or the foreign: the Italian *Vocabolario degli Accademici della Crusca*, 1612; the French *Dictionnaire de l'Académie Française*, 1694; the Spanish Academy's *Diccionario de la Lengua Española*, 1726–39.

Among the great foreign examples of lexicography in the nineteenth to twentieth centuries, we may—we should—cite at least the Grimm brothers' dictionary of German, begun in 1854 and still unfinished, and Littré's dictionary of French (1863–1878), perhaps the greatest of all the one-man dictionaries.

During the eighteenth to twentieth centuries, British and then American lexicography has made even more remarkable progress, landmarked by the following great works: Nathan Bailey's *Universal English Dictionary*, 1721, 4th edition 1728, with a considerable supplementary volume in 1731—it was upon these very notable books that Samuel Johnson based his justly famous dictionary of 1755 and with these that he had to compete, in general favour, right up to and during the 1780's; Noah Webster (the first great American lexicographer), *A Dictionary of the English Language*, 1828; Joseph Worcester, *A Dictionary of the English Language*, 1860—in this, the first dictionary to contain illustrations, Worcester proved that, although an active and very able lexicographer from 1829 onwards, he has been as unfairly overshadowed by Webster as Bailey by Johnson; *The Oxford English Dictionary*, edited by Sir James Murray, Dr Henry Bradley, Sir William Craigie and Dr C. T. Onions, 1884–1928, with Supplement in 1933— the greatest lexicographical undertaking, and achievement, of all time; 1909, *Webster's New International English Dictionary*, brilliantly revised, much enlarged, entirely re-set, 1934; Craigie and J. R. Hulbert, *A Dictionary of American English* (to 1900), 1936–44—a work shaped upon the O.E.D., yet showing many independent virtues; Mitford M. Mathews's differently notable *Dictionary of Americanisms* (up to 1950), 1951.

That bare recital of dictionaries fails, inevitably, to render justice to the high courage and the deep learning, the patience far beyond Penelope's, the faith, the sense of adventure, the selflessness, that have rendered possible such achievements as would cause 'the man in the street' to shudder and 'the woman in the home' to faint. Something of the labours endured, labours trickier than those of Tantalus and severer than those of Sisyphus, and something of these scholars' undimmed passion for learning, have been soberly described and modestly implied by Professor J. R. Hulbert in his compact, richly informative book, *Dictionaries, British and American*, 1954. A complete history of lexicography remains to be written; about the earliest period, however, much is available in *A History of Classical Scholarship* (1921), by Sir John Sandys.

CLICHÉS

In the year 1910, O. Henry's *Whirligigs*, a collection of short stories, contained one with the title 'Calloway's Code', based on the 'fact' that one H. B. Calloway, covering the Russo-Japanese war, sent to New York a cablegram written in code. The code was broken by an up-and-coming reporter named Vesey, who had the good sense to remember that newspapermen, like the rest of us, tend to fall back on those well-worn phrases which possess two remarkable virtues. They are readily *understood by even the meanest intelligence* and they cause the writer no pain at all.

Vesey deciphered the cable thus:

> 'Foregone—conclusion
> Preconcerted—arrangement
> Rash—act
> Witching—hour of midnight
> Goes—without saying
> Muffled—report
> Rumour—hath it
> Mine—host
> Dark—horse
> Silent—majority
> Unfortunate—pedestrians[1]
> Richmond—in the field
> Existing—conditions
> Great—White Way
> Hotly—contested
> Brute—force
> Select—few

[1] 'Mr Vesey afterward explained that the logical journalistic complement of the word "unfortunate" was once the word "victim". But, since the automobile became so popular, the correct following word is now "pedestrians". Of course, in Calloway's code it meant infantry.'

44

Mooted—question
Parlous—times
Beggars—description
Ye—correspondent
Angel—unawares
Incontrovertible—fact':

upon which Vesey comments: 'It's simply newspaper English
. . . I've been reporting on the *Enterprise* long enough to know
it by heart. Old Calloway gives us the cue word, and we use
the word that naturally follows it just as we use 'em in the
paper. Read it over, and you'll see how pat they drop into
their places.' The managing editor playfully jollied Vesey in a
few self-chosen words: 'Mr Vesey . . . you have cast a serious
reflection upon the literary standards of the paper that employs
you. You have also assisted materially in giving us the biggest
"beat" of the year.'

Of the ensuing success, O. Henry remarks: 'It was wonderful. And Calloway was wonderful. . . . And Vesey was wonderful. And most wonderful of all are words, and how they
make friends one with another, being oft associated, until not
even obituary notices do them part.' The ingenious Mr Vesey,
hearing that his salary has been raised, ends the story in this
satirical manner: 'All right. . . . Every little helps. Say—Mr
Scott, which would you say—"We can state without fear of
successful contradiction," or, "On the whole it can be safely
asserted"?'

Not even Frank Sullivan, in his delectable *New Yorker* skits
on clichés, has done better than O. Henry did so many years
ago. It's a pity that comparatively few contemporary journalists
and authors have read O. Henry—and that so many glibly
belittle him without the formality of reading him.

A year after O. Henry came out of prison, Edmund Gosse—
who usually talked sense, but who occasionally pontificated—
fulminated *in no uncertain terms*, as one might expect of *a citizen
of no mean city*, and, *believe it or not*, for the good of consulters of
The Encyclopaedia Britannica: 'All but the obvious motives tend
to express themselves no longer as thoughts but as clichés'.

Fifty-two years earlier than that, Tennyson had referred to the contemporary literary scene in the effective lines:

> 'And common is the commonplace
> And vacant chaff well meant for grain'.

And almost a century after Tennyson, that well-known London editor James Bone delivered himself of this ambiguous aphorism, 'To make a cliché is to make a classic', which I take to mean, 'Only something wise or witty or otherwise notable can end by becoming a cliché': a statement demonstrably true of certain kinds of cliché. (*Of which more anon.*)

The truth, I suspect, lies midway between Frank Binder's 'There is no bigger peril either to thinking or to education than the popular phrase' (*Dialectic*, 1932) and Frank Whitaker's verdict on clichés: 'Haste encourages them, but more often they spring from mental laziness' (an address to the Institute of Journalists, London, in 1938).

Observant readers will have noticed that I have encroached upon the domain of suspense-novelists by cheerfully quoting men either famous or, at the least, distinguished without having defined the term *cliché*. Let me still further abuse those readers' patience by mentioning the origin of the word. A *cliché* is 'something stereotyped', from French *clicher*, to stereotype, in the literal printing sense; it is an echoic word, related to French *claque* and to English *click* and *clack*.

That this elementary piece of etymology has not been thrown in for effect or as a jest will appear from the definitions given by the world's two best dictionaries of English: *The Oxford English Dictionary* and Webster's *New International Dictionary*. Whereas the former dismisses a cliché as 'a stereotyped expression, a commonplace phrase', the latter permits itself a more leisurely definition, 'A trite phrase that has lost precise meaning by iteration, a hackneyed or stereotyped expression'.

So now you know!—Or do you? Here I must compromise. Unless you're already authorities upon the subject of clichés—in which case you won't, unless you're very, very wise, be reading this article—you will not, for you cannot, have formed more than a vague idea of the nature and uses of clichés, for I have neither conscientiously shown the various types nor cited such examples as would have enabled you to form your own opinions. (I certainly do not expect you to accept mine.)

But before I can 'go all serious' I must yet be serious. After *more years than I care to remember* of noticing British and American clichés, I have been reluctantly forced to conclude that the addiction to clichés is far commoner than addiction to drugs and that the immense stock of clichés is common to both the United States and the British Commonwealth. Some clichés are less used in America than in Britain, some less in Britain than in America; but ninety-nine per cent of genuine, indisputable clichés are used in both countries. Indeed, the only All-American cliché I can put my pen on—and even this one isn't all that common in the U.S.A.—is the fairly recent *let the chips fall where they may*, which, by its very form, is clearly an educated specimen.

If one passes to the vogue-phrase, one can single out, here and there, a phrase employed in the one, not in the other, country. But these aren't strictly clichés, as may be gathered from the fact that they embody a turn, or a kind, of phrase rather than an expression. For instance, *came the dawn*—used in New York before appearing in London—initiated a group (*came the pay-off, came* this, *came* that, *came* the other) best exemplified perhaps by *came the reckoning*, which I've always suspected to be the earliest of them all. The *came the . . .* vogue has gone the way of all such vogues, thank heaven! It was a tiresome, too-literary, rather arty form, but it was worth mentioning, for it indicates one of the main differences between vogue-phrase and cliché: the majority of clichés last for generations, many for a century or even longer. Another difference is that the cliché is more 'human'—easily understood by all. Yet another, the cliché springs from the true, deep soil of language, the vogue-phrase from the top-soil. The cliché, in short, is natural, the vogue-phrase artificial.

But enough of dalliance by the wayside, pleasant though the wayside be, delightful though the dalliance. Consideration of the kinds of cliché will help us to understand its essential nature.

We may roughly classify clichés as belonging to one or other of four groups. It is worth noting that the second group often overlaps the first and that the fourth occasionally overlaps the third; also that the first two groups comprise at least four-fifths of the aggregate. All the same, it is the third and especially the fourth groups which offer the most interest and provide the most fun.

Group One consists of idioms that have become clichés; Group Two, of other hackneyed phrases. Group Three is formed of stock phrases and familiar quotations from foreign languages, and Group Four of quotations from English and American literature.

'Always define your terms' is a truism in logic, a truism applicable to all discourses and discussions. Do I hear someone ask, What exactly is an idiom? Nobody can give an exact definition. On the one hand, it may safely be stated that an idiom is a turn of phrase, a form of speech, peculiar to a people or a nation; on the other, and in a more particular sense, that it is always a form or a phrase approved by usage, and that sometimes it is a phrase with a total sense different from that of the sum of its parts and not always deducible from an understanding, even a weighing, of those parts. Idioms form an extremely important—an inseparable—part of a language; its very core, its essence, its last resort. But certain idioms have been so widely and so much used, often so indiscriminately used, that they have lost their freshness, their picturesqueness, their point; from being vivid metaphors they have become mere counters, a source of confusion, a recourse of sloppy thinkers. These idiom-clichés are familiar to and understood by everybody whose I.Q. is higher than that of a moron. They form the stock-in-trade of the morons, who, as often as not, don't firmly grasp their precise general meaning and thus debase them still further. Morons have nothing to say—but how persistently and ardently they say it! Although they propagate a pernicious type of cliché, yet one should charitably forgive them, for they have only one way—a means at once sole and pitiable—of 'making a noise in the world' and that is by making a hell of a lot of noise.

Idiom-clichés themselves are of various kinds: sub-species,

as it were. One of the largest is that of the doublets: *dust and ashes*—and *sackcloth and ashes*; *far and wide*; *for good and all*; *by leaps and bounds*; *much of a muchness* and *six of one and half a dozen of the other*; *null and void*; *heart and soul* and *tooth and nail* and *by hook and by crook*; *ways and means*; *to pick and choose*.

Then there's the repetition of a word, originally to secure emphasis, a purpose still vestigially visible in most of these clichés: *again and again* or *time and time again*; *through and through*; *share and share alike*. Often the device is more crafty or more literary, as in such alliterations as *bag and baggage, to chop and change, rack and ruin, safe and sound, slow but sure* (or *slow and sure*)— *with all one's might and main*; as in such rhymes as *fair and square* and *high and dry*; and as in such alternatives or complements or opposites as *ever and anon, fast and loose, for love or money, kill or cure, neither here nor there, the long and the short of it*.

Battered similes assault our sensibilities. From the multitude of such similes milling around us, we choose these few: *as steady as a rock* and *as old as the hills*—*as large as life* (occasionally elaborated to . . . *and twice as natural*, which Cuthbert Bede gave us as long ago as 1853)—*as fit as a fiddle*—*as cool as a cucumber*. But among the outworn metaphors, some are almost acceptable, perhaps because they derive either from trades and professions or from domestic life: witness *to know the ropes* and *leave the sinking ship*; *to stick to one's last*; *to set one's hand to the plough*; *to take potluck* and *lead a dog's life* and *to darken* (someone's) *door*.

Group Two consists of non-idiomatic hackneyed phrases: so exhausted with over-use that they can barely hold up their heads for shame. To allow oneself one of these, whether in writing or even in speech, is tantamount to resigning from the human race and to allying oneself with the monkeys and the parrots. Occasionally it may be not merely expedient but wise to heed the cynical dictum, 'If you cannot beat them, join 'em'; but that dictum certainly does not apply to the worst of all four kinds of cliché; here, if anywhere, looms *a fate worse than death*. Somewhere along the way, everyone must *call a halt* and *make a stand* and *resist to the bitter end*. *Death cometh soon or late*, and usually it comes quickly: but who could bear to live with himself after perpetrating and perpetuating such inanities, such trivialities, such approximations as those in the following list, deliberately drawn up in no particular order and kept mercifully brief—yet not so brief as to encourage the guilty to think they can 'get away with anything'.

To treat this, the most numerous, group proportionally would be to drive my readers to drink and me to despair. None of us would wish that. Here are a few, with a comment where necessary:

add insult to injury, which may originally have been a bad pun committed by a good etymologist;

any port in a storm (nautical);

baptism of fire (military);

at the eleventh hour (reprieve);

explore every avenue (almost the silliest cliché) and *leave no stone unturned*—two of the commonest;

fall on deaf ears;

grow no younger;

halcyon days (from an Ancient Greek myth);

imagination runs riot and *imagination boggles;*

a moot point (properly, one for discussion);

nip in the bud (frosts);

the open road;

the picture of health;

at the psychological moment (via French from German; horribly misunderstood and misused);

runs in the blood (hereditary);

the salt of the earth (from the New Testament);

sick at heart;

skate on thin ice;

the (very) soul of honour;

the staff of life (not quite so nauseatingly overworked as it used to be);

a superhuman effort (compare the candidate *superhuman energy*);

twelve good men and true (but sometimes not very bright);

venture an opinion (one of the least offensive);

welcome with open arms and then *speed the parting guest;*

you could have knocked me down with a feather—a fate much too good for the perpetrator.

Some of the political and sociological clichés are so revolting and so often mouthed with such intolerable unction that no conscientious castigator should fail to list a few. Perhaps the following are as objectionable as any:

to leave a (or *the*) *door open* for further futile committees;
the march of time (compare the general *How time flies!*);
laying heretical hands upon our imperishable constitution (far more American than British);
maintain the status quo (slightly more British than American);
learn from a reliable source.

Thus we pass, *not without a sigh of relief*, to the Third Group: phrases and quotations from either dead or foreign languages. Only by very well-read people are any Greek phrases used as clichés. But a few Latin phrases do qualify; for instance, *ceteris paribus* (other thing being equal)—*de mortuis*, followed by a most eloquent pause that indicates the remainder, *nil nisi bonum*, Of the dead, speak charitably—*deus ex machina* (theatrical in origin)—*in flagrante delicto*, caught right in the act—*longo intervallo*, after a long interval—*mutatis mutandis*, allowing for the necessary changes or modifications—*persona grata* and *pro bono publico*, both familiar to even a Philistine. Of the French, the best known are these:

bête noire (far too often misspelt), a bugbear;
carte blanche, a free hand;
cherchez la femme;
fait accompli;
(un) je ne sais quoi, something indescribable;
toujours la politesse.

Of the French quotations properly so called, these two clamour for inclusion: *Nous avons changé tout cela*, as, 'way back in 1666, Molière declared, only to be contradicted, in 1849, by Alphonse Karr, *Plus ça change, plus c'est la même chose*, usually misquoted as . . . *plus ça reste la même chose.*

Naturally, the clichés that consist of quotations from British and American authors are so numerous that one *simply doesn't know where to begin*. Fortified by that profession of faith, I list, with a random nonchalance that will very properly infuriate the righteous, a few quotations that stand very high in any right-minded scale of popularity.

Probably the most famous quotation, not only in our two countries but throughout the literate world, is that Shakespearean passage from *Hamlet* which commences: 'To be or not to be: that is the question'. But then, as an enlightened schoolboy once remarked, *Hamlet* is full of quotations. (Nearly as full are *Lear* and *Macbeth* and *Othello*.) But the quotation that deserves to be the best known of all comes, not from English or American literature, but from an English translation from Hebrew. In the Authorized Version or King James's Bible, it reads: 'Be still, and know that I am God'—which lies at the heart of all religion and which has not become a cliché. Another very famous Biblical quotation, this time a notorious cliché, is *Their name is Legion*, utterly misunderstood by nine hundred and ninety-nine in every thousand. Almost as tattered and battered are Milton's *dim religious light* and Keats's *A thing of beauty is a joy for ever*. The oddest quotation-clichés are those which have turned into clichés only in misquotations, such as— to select but one—*When Greek meets Greek*, often completed . . . *then comes the tug-of-war*; what Nathaniel Lee wrote in 1677 was 'When Greeks joined Greeks [that is, engaged them in battle], then was the tug-of-war'.

Perhaps the only American rivals of those English quotations are several occurring in Longfellow. (We have to omit Benjamin Franklin's proverbs, because proverbs cannot fairly be called clichés.) Clichés in Britain no less than in America are these two from *A Psalm of Life*:

> 'Tell me not, in mournful numbers,
> Life is but an empty dream!'

> 'Life is real! Life is earnest!'

Line for line, this Longfellow poem contains more passages that have become clichés than any other poem—than, indeed, any other literary work.

'That's all very well! But are we never to use clichés at all? Aren't they sometimes—well, perhaps not justifiable, but at least excusable?' A fair question.

> 'To cleesh or not to cleesh: that is the question:
> Whether it is nobler in the mind to suffer
> The dread commonplaces of outrageous morons,
> Or to take pen against a sea of clichés,
> And by opposing end them?
> For who would bear the quipping, boring fools. . . .
> When he himself might his defiance make
> With a bare "*No!* no!"?'

To begin with, I'd declare that clichés are never necessary, for nobody is either ethically or legally or, come to that, logically obliged to employ them. I should prefer not to be found dead with one, although I probably shall be; but that doesn't mean to say that I'm such a dim, dull, dedicated, desperate pedant that I won't admit that very often the primary consideration is not stylistic nor even linguistic. Clearly there arise situations, precisely as there exist conditions, in which, whether confronted by peril or some other extreme urgency or harrowed by horror or stricken with grief, one has to say *some*thing: when the sheer need for utterance far outweighs the merely secondary advisability of elegant, or even of lucid, speech; when, indeed, the latter becomes an impropriety, an irrelevance, a stupidity—or worse, an inhumanity. Politicians and other public speakers have been known to justify the cliché by saying that they naturally wish, that they are even bound to, employ phrases that will—or so the optimistic fellows hope—be understood by the entire audience, the implication being that clichés are familiar to everyone. Now and then, warnings have to be given promptly and emphatically; obviously there's no time to search either for the right word and the best phrase, or for clarity and precision, however desirable clarity and precision may be. The clear-minded man, like an able speaker, succeeds better than the man who is neither; yet the latter is at least putting *first things first*, always an admirable rule. Sincerity, after all, is what is needed most: to the sincere, we can and should excuse much.

Perhaps we might summarize the pros and cons for and against clichés in some such way as this. In the interplay of conversation, a cliché is often redeemed by a moue or a shrug or an accomplice-smile: 'There! I've used a cliché. Very careless and humdrum of me, I suppose. But at least you know what I mean.' Intonation, pauses, emphasis, these and other means can invest a cliché-ridden sentence, or set of sentences, with humour and wit, and with realism and trenchancy. In writing, we lack these dramatic, these theatrical, these extraneous aids: we *stand or fall alone*. In writing, the battered simile and the forgotten metaphor may well be ludicrous or inept or repellent; the hackneyed phrase so commonplace that it offends, the idiom so weak that it enfeebles the argument or dulls the description or obscures the statement; the foreign phrase either so inadequate or so out of place that it sets up a misgiving, a doubt, a dissent; the quotation so mauled by the maudlin, so coy in the mouths of the prim, so bombastic in the speech of the pompous, as to be risible, so very common as to lose all distinction, so inept as to fail.

'If in doubt, don't!'

A SQUARE DIGS BEATNIK

Beatnik is the 'language'—partly slang, partly jargon—spoken by *Beatniks*, as the San Franciscan press christened members of the *Beat* community or fraternity living in the North Beach area; a community that has focused American attention upon *the Beat generation*. Those who wish to know more of the community cannot do better than to read Lady Caroline Freud's brilliant 'Portrait of the Beatnik' in the June 1959 issue of *Encounter*; those interested in the background will, in the August number of that very intelligent periodical, find an idealized and mythopoetic sketch entitled 'Beatific: On the Origins of a Generation', written by Jack Kerouac, author of *On the Road*, which, issued in 1957, explained both him and the very vague movement which he characterizes and, to some extent, leads. But there's plenty of room at the top.

Whereas *Beatnik* merely adds *-nik* (as in *Sputnik*) to *Beat*, 'the *Beat* Generation' isn't quite so easy to determine. In an article published in 1952, *The New York Times* (Sunday Magazine) referred to Kerouac as saying 'This is a Beat Generation'; slowly this designation made its way; in 1955, Kerouac's article 'Jazz of the Beat Generation' accelerated its acceptance; *On the Road* finally canonized 'the *Beat* Generation', a fact pinpointed by a film of *The Beat Generation*, shown in mid-1959. By that time, there already existed three origins: earliest, the *beat*en or down-trodden generation, which Mr Kerouac indignantly and justly repudiates, for it's nothing of the sort, whether sociologically or linguistically; latest, the *beat*ific generation, an opinion Mr Kerouac in his article and elsewhere has been doing his darnedest to impose upon all us simple squares, an origin no less incorrect and inaccurate and inadequate than the earliest; and the generation that adores the *beat* or rhythm of jazz and its various developments and modifications, an origin supported by a mass of evidence so impressive that a mere square wonders how either of the other two explanations could have gained a moment's credence.

Beatnik, the special vocabulary of Beatniks, has been described by Lady Caroline Freud as 'a code' based upon language reduced to a minimum and consisting of 'an abbreviated version of already abbreviated Jazz talk'. Its brevity, tending (the square thinks) rather to obscurity than to wit, depends much upon context; but then, so does all language. This vocabulary springs from four sources: general American slang; the language of jazz musicians and *aficionados*; the Beatniks themselves, who, with such writers as Jack Kerouac and Alan Ginsberg, Kenneth Rexroth and Lawrence Kipton, prominent in the arcane oligarchy that directs or tries to direct the movement, do not lack originality; and, both fundamentally and numerically, much less influential than any of the other sources, the underworld.

It is so difficult to separate the words of specifically Beatnik origin from those arising elsewhere, that a mere 'Limey square' would be stupid to attempt the task, except to note *wail*, to live, stay alive, subsist, function, perhaps suggested by the idea of existence in 'this wail of tears'. Of the 'general American slang' group, I need mention only two: *chick*, a girl, a young woman; *drop!*, for *drop dead!* (go away and stop bothering me). The terms deriving from jazz are numerous. How numerous can be perhaps guessed, almost gauged, from Professor Norman Hinton's statement made in a sane, well-balanced, instructive article, 'The Language of Jazz Musicians' in the American Dialect Society's Publication dated November 1958 but appearing in May 1959: 'The basic terms, as I see them, are *cat, cool, crazy, dig, end, goof, hip, jazz, man, most, square,* and *swing*'. (*Man,* however, is a mere vocative, as in 'Go, man, go!') Many other Beatnik terms likewise originated in jazz. The underworld element has been ignored by Lady Caroline Freud and Mr Kerouac and also by Mr Andrew MacFarlane, the witty author of 'Basic Beatnik (A Square's Guide to Hip Talk)' in the 16 April 1959 issue of *The Daily Colonist* (Victoria, British Columbia).

Both that underworld element and the other three will

emerge clearly enough in the following list of thirteen-or-so terms that, in addition to *Beat* and *Beatnik*, have been selected for more than a cursory reference: *square; dig; hip* (and *hipster*) with its originator, *hep; cool* and *cool cat* and, indeed, *something else; go* and *gone; crazy; (the) most; swing*, with *swingin'; way out; hang-up* and *pad*, noun and verb.

Among jazz musicians, *square* means 'not in accordance with the jazzman's aesthetic standards. Probably comes from steady 1-2-3-4 rhythm without variation. Many musicians, while saying the word, will make a motion similar to the band director's indication for 4/4 time—the hand moves in a square for the four beats' (Hinton). Among Beatniks it means either anyone not a Beatnik or 'someone who doesn't dig' (*Colonist*). In general slang it means either anyone ignorant or unappreciative of jazz or even an unmusical, uncultured, unlettered person. In the underworld, the adjective denotes 'honest' and the noun occurs only as *the square*, fair, honest, upright dealing and living; both noun and adjective were current in England at least a generation before they crossed the Atlantic. Hence the tendency, whether in the U.S.A. and Canada or in Britain, for the noun *square* to stigmatize, among Beatniks and jazz-lovers and Teddy boys, any ordinary upright citizen of decent morals; 'Don't be a square' often conveys no more than 'Don't be stuffy'.

'To *dig*' is understood by jazz musicians as 'to understand and agree with: not limited to music alone. (Perhaps from a sense of "getting to the bottom" of things)' (Hinton). Among Beatniks it is either 'to know, become aware of' (*Colonist*) or 'to agree, to acquiesce' (Lady Caroline Freud). In general American and Canadian slang it covers such nuances as 'to observe; to observe and understand; to observe and admire or, at the least, appreciate'. British 'con men' earlier used it for 'to make inquiries and contacts'.

Hip is, by jazz musicians, applied to one 'in the know' or 'of the élite' and it can be employed for 'to understand', where the Beatnik sense is 'equipped with enough wisdom, philosophy and courage to be self-sufficient, independent of society; able to swing on any scene' (a place where anything happens):

Colonist. Anyone—especially the Beatnik—who is *hip* becomes thereby a *hipster* (Kerouac). *Hip* is a 'thinning' of the older *hep*, which, by the way, has regained favour among jazz musicians (Hinton). The term comes from the American underworld, where *hep* and later *hip* signify 'shrewd and alert, or well-informed, or all three', and perhaps derives from a teamster's *hep! hep!* as a call of encouragement to horses—the horses themselves *getting hep*.

Cool occurs mostly in *cool cat*, as in 'Dig that cool cat!' and implies a laudable detachment or moderation or poise; *cat*, now simply 'a fellow', was, among jazz musicians of the 1930's, one who was 'hep'; earlier still, the American underworld applied *cat* either to a tramp new to the road or to an itinerant worker existing on the fringes of tramp society, and *gay cat* (*ca*. 1880–1920) to either a tramp on the move or a dilettante tramp or an inexperienced tramp. A 'cat' may be so 'cool' as to defy description: he's *something else*.

Praise is expressed also by *way out*, 'enigmatic and abstract' (Freud); *crazy*, 'fabulously interesting, great' (*Colonist*) or, among jazz musicians, 'like *cool* and almost interchangeable with it' (Hinton)—compare those musicians' *the most* and *the greatest*; *(real) gone*, inspired or exhilarated by music, and *go!*, 'dig, get with it, swing', belong to both jazz and Beatnik; *swingin'*, which, among jazz musicians, is a most laudatory adjective, comes from their *swing*, 'to play well in all senses . . . but especially to have the basic feel for jazz rhythms' (Hinton), whence, in turn, the Beatnik *swing*, 'to get the feel of, to comprehend the truth and beauty of anything worth digging; to impart the same truth or beauty to others' (*Colonist*).

Common to—indeed, very common in—the jazzmen's and the Beatniks' vocabulary is the noun *pad*, whence the entirely Beatnik *pad me*, a cat's invitation to a chick to share his room and bed. *Pad* is 'a bed. Extended to mean bedroom, or even apartment' (Hinton)—'living quarters, often a bare room with a mattress on or near the floor' (*Colonist*)—'home where he keeps his foam rubber mattress' (Freud). The Beatniks got it from the jazzmen who got it from the American underworld who got it from the British underworld (*pad*, a bed) who got it from Standard English of the sixteenth to eighteenth centuries (*pad*, a bundle of straw to lie on).

Perhaps so meagre a selection of Beatnik leaves an entirely false impression. The subject merits a serious and erudite monograph by someone more nearly *with it* than ever I could hope to be.

(Written in August, 1959.)

IN MEMORIAM

HENRY WATSON FOWLER [1]

THE majority of people have nothing to say, and keep on saying it. Henry Watson Fowler had much to say, but most of us wish he had said more on almost every subject he touched. Nor did he confine himself to the vast field of English language. He did not, like Goldsmith, adorn every subject he treated: he did better than that: he enriched and illuminated it.

H. W. Fowler, who died on Boxing Day, 1933, and the centenary of whose birth falls on March 10 of this year,[2] was a very different person from what most of his readers have imagined him. It is true that for seventeen years he taught in what we English so oddly call a Public School and that 'once a teacher, always a teacher'; but he was the very best kind of teacher, a notable member of that selfless profession to which we owe so much and treat so shabbily. He possessed exceptional physical and moral courage and that much rarer quality, fortitude. Like his distinguished contemporary, C. E. Montague, he falsified his age (fifty-seven) by many years in order to serve in France during World War One, not as an officer on a gilded staff but in the ranks and the trenches. He had an inexhaustible sense of fun, a rich sense of humour, a pleasant wit. Always kindly and considerate to others, he himself lived a simple, indeed a spartan, life. When, after the war, he settled down to lexicographical work in the service of perhaps the most generous of all publishers, the Oxford University Press offered to provide him with a servant, so that his Somersetshire cottage might be left free for him to enjoy it and his work. His reply, at the age of sixty-eight and in the month of November, is famous in English academic circles but little known elsewhere: 'My half-hour from 7 to 7.30 this morning was spent in (1) a two-mile run along the road, (2) a swim in my next-door neighbour's

---

[1] *The New York Times*, March 10, 1958, in a slightly shorter version.
[2] 1958.

63

pond. . . . That I am still in condition for such freaks I attribute
to having had for nearly thirty years no servants to reduce me
to a sedentary and all-literary existence. And now you seem to
say: Let us give you a servant, and the means of slow suicide
and quick lexicography.' On his fiftieth birthday he married;
after an unfashionably happy marriage, of twenty-two years, his
wife pre-deceased him by four years. Everywhere he went, he
inspired not only respect, but affection; not only admiration,
but liking, whether among scholars and students, as was
natural, or among all other sorts and conditions of men and
women.

Henry Watson Fowler (1858–1933) was a great man. He was
also, in the best sense and in the best ways, a very good man.
This 'merely moral man' put most professing Christians to
shame.

All his life, Fowler worked hard and carefully. He scorned
the slipshod and the shoddy alike. He paid his readers a compli-
ment few could have deserved, for he had a first-rate mind and
all his work is first-rate. Even as a versifier (he knew that he
wasn't a poet) he wrote with clarity and charm; as an essayist,
he wrote with clarity and charm and distinction, although
without success.

In the earlier half of his writing life, H. W. Fowler mostly
collaborated with his brother Francis, who, born in 1870, died
in 1918 as a delayed result of privations on the Western Front.
Excellent Classical scholars, the two brothers began in 1903 and
published in 1905 the best of all translations of that Greek
satirist Lucian who set the fashion in 'dialogues of the dead'.
A year later, they issued a famous work, *The King's English*,
revised finally by H. W. alone in 1930 and still used by the
older generation of teachers and students and deserving to be
used more freely by the younger generation. Much as, a very
few years later, Ernest Weekley got the idea of his famous series
of books on words from Archbishop Richard Chenevix Trench's
On the Study of Words, 1851 (14th edition, 1872), and *English,
Past and Present*, 1855 (10th edition, 1877), works that retained
their popularity until Weekley's superseded them, so the
brothers Fowler owed the idea of their astringently corrective

book to Dean Henry Alford's *The Queen's English*, which published in 1864, had reached its seventh edition in 1888 and was still being used right up to 1906, when *The King's English*— a much better book—killed it stone dead. *The King's English*, although existing and thriving in its own right, has often been regarded as a *ballon d'essai* for *A Dictionary of Modern English Usage*, despite the fact that the earlier work, succeeding beyond the authors' hopes, merely gave them the idea for the later and greater work.

But twenty years intervened between the first publication of *The King's English* and that of *Modern English Usage*. Apart from the disruption caused by recruiting, by soldiering, by munitions work, most of that period of H. W. Fowler's life was occupied in lexicography for the Oxford University Press, especially on *The Concise Oxford Dictionary of Current English*. Appearing in 1923, 'The Concise Oxford'—as it is affectionately known— was, initially, the work of the two brothers. Revised, it has retained its place, almost immediately won, as the best concise dictionary of English for scholars, students, teachers, authors, journalists, and for all others whose tastes are literary and artistic rather than scientific or technological. It combines precision and elegance.

Francis Fowler had no hand in the writing of *Modern English Usage* (M.E.U., as scholars call it), but he did help H. W. to plan the work and to get it under way. This world-famous book contains a moving and eloquent memorial dedication to the younger man, a dedication remarkable for the attribution to Francis of 'a nimbler wit, a better sense of proportion, and a more open mind, than his twelve-year-older partner'; which, in its generous exaggeration, recalls the praise accorded by Edmond de Goncourt (1827–96) to his younger brother Jules, who had, at the age of forty, pre-deceased him by a quarter of a century.

When *Modern English Usage* appeared in 1926, I was a very junior lecturer in the University of Manchester, a fact I mention only to show that, surrounded by a university's staff and students, I was in a position to note and enjoy the stir made by this austere work. Students and other irreverent persons

3

delighted in Fowler's pillorying, both of *The Times* and other important periodicals and of celebrated writers: 'and' (to adapt a passage from *The Song of Songs*) 'the voice of the victim was heard in the land'. Fowler had decided upon this courageous course, not in order to puncture this reputation or that, nor yet to show how clever he was (after all, he possessed so very much more than mere cleverness), but simply in order to perform a public service. The louder and more numerous were the outcries, the more appreciatively did the general intelligent public savour the dry wine that was M.E.U.

Even before his death, Fowler became a legend; a legend he has remained. As always happens after a great man's death, and so soon as a decent interval has been allowed to elapse, the jackals and the hyenas first insinuated and then asserted that M.E.U. contains many faults. Of course it does! Every worthwhile book contains many faults, and every worth-while writer commits them. Look how shockingly incorrect is much of Shakespeare's English! But, on a major issue, only once did Fowler err: and that was because his sense of logic overcame his sense of usage. Jespersen attacked Fowler for his article on 'the fused participle'; Fowler replied; the honours went to Jespersen. This was odd, for Fowler had the better sense and knowledge of usage, Jespersen the better sense and knowledge of grammar. Also, the error was entirely unnecessary, for Dr C. T. Onions had, twenty-two years earlier in his *Advanced English Syntax*, conclusively shown that both usages, the one defended and the one condemned by Fowler, were correct and that it is the context which determines which of the two is preferable on any given occasion. There does, however, exist one very serious objection to *Modern English Usage*. Even when it appeared, the book was slightly out of date.

Let me explain that apparent heresy! In its principles and, with one exception, its precepts, M.E.U. is impeccable: its teachings have proved invaluable: they still are. But Fowler sometimes failed to notice what was happening in post-war English; his theory seemed to rest, in the main, upon the practice of the writers of (roughly) 1890–1914. For instance, the section on *as if* and *as though* is very good, so far as it goes; it doesn't go far enough, for he neglects to mention the distinctions involved. To me, M.E.U. has always been a grand book to consult; yet it has always impressed me with a sense of unreality. To say that it contains only counsels of perfection would be to exaggerate, yet it does contain very little else. Its slight archaism, its decided perfectionism, its pervasive and disquieting unreality do not prevent it from being the best book of its kind ever written in any European language. Because I felt that there was room for a less ambitious but more truly and immediately contemporaneous work, I wrote *Usage and Abusage*, and I've kept it up to date. The first publisher to whom I submitted the idea refused the book, on the grounds that 'to compete with Fowler would be to commit suicide' and 'Fowler is too well established'; because I wasn't competing with him, and because I have constantly improved and 'modernized' my book, I've succeeded to an extent that still amazes me.

Fowler's *Modern English Usage*, never revised by Fowler, is, we are told, being revised by a committee of scholars. But wouldn't it have been wiser to leave M.E.U. as it was, without superimpositions on the idiosyncrasies, the integrity, the authoritativeness and, above all, the uniformity that made it what it was, a remarkable and genuinely original masterpiece? I adore Fowler, but this side revision—well this side external revision by a team. There is only one Fowler. I, for one, shall be sad to lose him.

H. L. MENCKEN

An Appreciation: 1956

H. L. MENCKEN, who has died at the age of 75, remained throughout his life an *enfant terrible*, particularly in criticism (whether of life or of literature) and in his writings (whether ephemeral or permanent) on language, especially on 'the American language'—as he persisted in calling it. Although a virile and brilliant journalist and a distinguished and vigorous editor, a prolific and versatile essayist, forceful and immensely readable, an idiosyncratic anthologist of quotations, a trenchant satirist of religion, he worked best in the field of language, where his most enduring work was done. He took something less than pleasure or, at most, a somewhat rueful pleasure in the American journalistic description of him as 'The Sage of Baltimore', where he was born, where he mainly lived even during the most active years, and where he lived after his retirement from the editorship of *The American Mercury*; despite the *panache* he sported with the insouciance of an undergraduate and the picturesqueness of a buccaneer, he was fundamentally a modest, even a humble man.

In his latter years, he came also to take little pleasure in the reputation he had gained of being the entirely convinced and the truculently convincing champion of American speech and language; but then, he had always said some extremely rude things about American culture and, indeed, about American civilization as a whole. During the last fifteen or so years, he was steadily becoming far less intransigent in his belief that American English was, at every point and in every way, superior to English and that English was doomed to become little more than a dialect, vestigial and quaint and ever more rapidly decadent, with the natural concomitant that, as this decay was taking place, American English would gradually be achieving

68

a complete supremacy, to the great benefit of Britain and of the world. I doubt whether this gallant attitude ever did attain to the status of a belief, much less to that of a dogma. Certainly, on this subject as on so many others, he was much more cautious, infinitely more urbane and tolerant, in his private pronouncements than in his public. The loudness of the American bark notably exceeded the severity of the bite at the delicate British anatomy.

The American Language appeared first in 1918; a considerably enlarged edition came out in 1923; the third, likewise corrected and considerably enlarged, a few years later; the fourth or definitive edition in 1936 (as he once confided, he felt that it was time to 'call it a day')—by now the book was hardly recognizable. Yet he could not abandon the subject: why, after all, should he? But he left untouched *The American Language* proper and contented himself with writing two huge supplements: *Supplement One* appearing in 1945; *Supplement Two* in 1948. These Supplements served the triple purpose of enriching subjects already treated—of keeping up to date—and of discovering and illuminating fresh aspects and new vistas.

In appraising Mencken's *magnum opus*—for *The American Language* is precisely that, both physically and intellectually— we have to bear in mind three basic facts. First, intensely American, he upheld the theory of 'my country, right or wrong', and, although he often knew and, in fact, said that it was wrong, he disliked others saying so. Secondly, he was, by training, not an academic but a journalist—a journalist with literary aspirations, but a first-rate all-round journalist. Thirdly, he grew up in a moral climate of agnosticism—when it wasn't atheism— and often he shocked the conventional with the frankness of his animadversions upon religion and even upon ethics; he was, however, far from being the 'tough *hombre*' he so enjoyed pretending to be. All the moral and intellectual hardness lay on the surface of this likable and admirable, this dynamic and remarkable personality.

Believing so whole-heartedly in the industrial, commercial, financial greatness of the United States of America and in its intellectual and moral qualities as well, he inevitably believed in the robustness, the ability to survive—more, in the superiority and destined predominance—of the spoken and written language.

Being essentially a journalist, constantly exercising himself in narrative and descriptive, persuasive and expository English, he regarded American English not as a subject for unremittingly critical dissection and for philosophical synthesis, but as a matter of abiding and enthralling interest. Professor John W. Clark, an American and part-author of *A History of British and American English since 1950*, has drawn attention, both to the fact that Mencken was so absorbed in his passion for the *trees* of language that he sometimes lost sight of the *wood* or forest, and to the associated fact that he perhaps too consistently emphasized the particular, the strange and the odd, the superficial and the ephemeral, at the expense of the general, the everyday, the enduring and the fundamental. This is true. Nevertheless, a careful reading of, and a pondered judgement on, *The American Language* will reveal that, in the main, H. L. Mencken's abundance of luxuriant detail was intentional: only thus, he held, could he bring out the supreme merits of American English— its liveliness, its picturesqueness, its astounding vigour, its untiring inventiveness, its amazing ability to hit upon the right word.

Being a genuine agnostic, being moreover a militant and at times rather arrogant agnostic, Mencken neglected the spiritual aspects of language in general and of American English in particular. Fortunately for him—and for us—that defect in his make-up had far fewer and much less important consequences than might have been feared, for he did not pretend— indeed, he had not intended—to write a history either aesthetic or spiritual.

It was in the historical parts of his book, and also in certain articles for encyclopaedias and for literary periodicals, that Mencken expressed most freely and with the deepest prejudice his anti-British feelings. That he himself knew he was prejudiced we perceive from the fact that he was obsessed with the very word *prejudice*. From some ultimately creditable, deeply-seated, ineradicable sense of independence, he resented the implicit, the undeniable element and very basis of English (that is, *native* or British English) in American English: he was not a *Mayflower* man: he was of Central European extraction. In short, when he denied the vastly predominant Englishness of American English, he was not denying his birthright. On the contrary, he was postulating, asserting, proclaiming that new birth of English which we call American English. No Englishman, no Scot, no Welshman, no Irishman, no Briton in the Dominions and the Colonies, thinks the less of Mencken for his—whatever is the American equivalent of 'jingoism' or 'chauvinism' or 'irredentism'.

Besides being an unyielding, dyed-in-the-wool American and, in his own unusual way, a great writer, Henry Louis Mencken was certainly a great man: as loyal to his colleagues and his friends as to the causes he selflessly and nobly upheld; compact of honesty and honour, and of an immaculate integrity; overflowing with kindliness and generosity, occasionally too well disguised as irascibility; of a steel-tempered courage during the last seven paralysed years, a courage accompanied by the rarer gift of fortitude: in short, a man of good will, of enlightenment, of true sweetness and lovableness of character.

America has lost a true son; the world, a true friend.

MEDICINE,
PSYCHIATRY, THE ESOTERIC

3*

THE ETYMOLOGY OF MEDICINE

'. . . AND for the purposes of this Act, *medicine* is to be taken in its widest meaning, with no nonsense about medical and surgical wards.'

From its very nature and supreme importance, medicine has a vocabulary rich in words with long and fascinating etymologies or histories, perhaps none more notable than that of *medicine* itself, which came into Middle English from Old French *medecine*, from Latin *medicina*, an *-ina* derivative from *medic*us, a physician, an *-icus* derivative (originally adjectival, from Greek *-ikos*, the commonest of adjectival suffixes) from *medēri*, to heal, a doctor being primarily a healer: and *med-* is that Indo-European base or root *med-*, variant *met-*, which, meaning 'to measure, hence to consider', appears in L *medi*tari, to meditate (literally to measure in one's mind), L *met*ire, to measure, Old English *met*an, to measure: a doctor can heal a sick person only after he has *measured* the nature and extent of the complaint and then *considered* what is to be done about it. L *medicus*, physician, becomes Italian *medico*, adopted by English as an endearing term of familiar reference, and acquires the adjective *medicalis*, our *medical*.

The general practitioner of medicine has long been known as *doctor*. This sense has triumphed over the two that, in the Middle Ages, co-existed on equal terms: 'doctor of philosophy' and 'doctor of theology', which survive only in academic circles. *Doctor* has come through French from L *doctor*, a teacher, from *docēre*, to teach; among the most famous European physicians, surgeons, professors of medicine, have always been those of Paris. Nowadays, a doctor concerning himself with medicine as opposed to surgery is a *physician*, Middle English—from Old French—*fisicien*, from L *physica*, from Gr *phusikē*, short for *phusikē tekhnē*, skill (hence art and science) in or of Nature, hence natural science, from *phus*is, Nature, from *phu*ein, to produce, to

75

cause to emerge into existence and to grow. Like *doctor*, *physician* has become specialized.

The doctor concerning himself with the treatment of either injury (or deformity) or disease by manual or instrumental—strictly, manual and instrumental—operations, is a *surgeon*, Middle English *surgien*, a contraction of Old French *serurgien*, a variant of *cirurgien*, an *-ien* derivative (compare Old French *fisicien*) from *cirurgie*, variant *serurgie*, from late Latin *chirurgia*, from Greek *kheirourgia*, an *ourgia* (from *ergein*, to work) or working with the *kheir* or hand : a manual skill, indeed the noblest of all manual skills. It is pertinent to recall that the *kheir* is fundamentally 'the grasper' and that *operation*, so ominous a word to many laymen, means simply 'a working', through French from Latin *operatio* ('of an operation' being *operationis*), from *operari*, to work, from *opus*, work, akin to the synonymous Sanskrit *ápas*, probably of religious origin.

All medical *treatment* is designed to *cure* the sufferer. *Treatment* derives from French *traitement*, from *traiter* (whence to *treat*), from Latin *tractare*, to handle, itself the frequentative of *trahere*, to draw or pull along (*tractus*, drawn or pulled) ; here, as in *surgery*, the emphasis rests upon manual skill. A *cure*, whence 'to *cure*', comes, as the majority of medical terms come, through French : and the Old French *cure* derives from Latin *cura*, anxiety or sorrow, hence care, the trouble one takes, especially for others, from an Indo-European basic word meaning 'to sorrow' : *cure*, therefore, expresses that selfless care which characterizes physicians and surgeons alike.

Doctors are often assisted by *nurses*; doctors often work in *hospitals*. Both *nurse* and *hospital* are words possessing a history longer and more interesting and more fundamentally important than that possessed by most of the technicalities of the other professions.

A *nurse*, Middle English from Old French *norice*, or ME *nurice* from OF *nurrice*, draws her name from Late Latin *nutricia*, a nurse, a noun formed from the feminine of the Latin adjective *nutricius*, applied to one who nourishes, especially one who suckles a baby, from *nutrix*, a wet nurse, itself from *nutrire*, to nourish, especially to wet-nurse a baby, to suckle it (compare 'a *nursing* mother'). The root of *nutrire* is *nu-*, akin to the *na-* of Greek *naein*, to flow, and to the *nau-* of Sanskrit *snauti*, she gives milk, a word containing that prefix *s-* which we see in Greek *stegos*, a roof, a house, as compared with its virtual synonym, *tegos*, and in *snow* (Old English *snaw*) as compared with Latin *niuis*, of snow. Here, then, we find yet another specialization of sense; occurring, this time, so long ago as in Late Latin; that is, during the approximate period A.D. 180–600.

Hospital has a story rather differently complex from that of *nurse*. In its archaic shortened form *spital*, it occurs in *Spitalfields* and in the now only historically famous *Spital* of London. The word *hospital* came into English from Old French; OF *hospital* represents Medieval Latin *hospitale*, properly the neuter of the Latin adjective *hospitalis*, relating to a *hospes* or guest (in Late Latin, an innkeeper); *hospitale* was apparently suggested by the L *hospitalis domus*, a house for the reception of guests. The medieval monasteries and convents gave food and shelter to travellers and, to the needy, alms and, to the ill, care: the passage from such a 'guest-house' to a hostel for the sick and the aged, thence to a hospital in the modern sense, is linguistically normal and culturally inevitable. In Latin, *hospes* was both the receiver and entertainer of strangers, i.e. the host, and the stranger received, i.e. the guest. *Hospes* (stem *hosp-*, root *hos-*) is intimately related to *hostis* (stem *host-*, root *hos-*), a foreigner or a stranger, hence a guest, with the latter sense gradually ousted by *hospes* and with the equally natural sense 'enemy' simultaneously coming to predominate, so that *hospitalis* means only 'hospitable' and *hostilis* only 'inimical, hostile'. It looks, therefore, as if both *hospes* and *hostis* descend from a remote Indo-European root *hos-*, a stranger. And, by the way, that Medieval Latin *hospitale*, which gave us *hospital*, also gives us, again through Old French, *hostel*, where the 'guest-house' sense has survived, partly because of the 'true hospital' competition set up by *hospital*.

Of the many other medical terms clamouring for inclusion— one could so easily write a considerable monograph upon medical etymologies!—a few of those for anaesthetics and drugs stand out as perhaps the most generally interesting. *Anaesthetic* (noun from adjective) imitates *aesthetic* and derives from Greek *anaisthētos*, unfelt, hence unfeeling, insensible; *drug*, formerly with a much wider application, comes, through Middle English *drogge*, from Old French *drogue*, itself from Low German *droge vate*, dry vats or casks, in which *droge*, dry, was wrongly thought to refer to the contents. Consequently *drug* is ultimately the same word as *dry* and akin to *drought*.

A very ancient drug is *opium*, a Latin word from Greek *opion*, juice of that poppy which yields opium; from *opos*, any vegetable juice. The more powerful *morphine*, one of those innumerable chemical and medical derivatives in *-ine*, is adopted from French, which takes it from German *Morphin*, which comes, through Latin, from *Morpheus*, the Greek god of dreams (not, as so commonly stated, of sleep), literally 'The Shaper or Fashioner', from the shapes he evokes for the dreamer, *Morpheus* deriving from *morphē*, shape, form. (*Morphia* is a Scientific Latin alteration of the earlier *morphium*, itself from *Morph*eus.) A similarly German-named drug is *heroin*, Ger *Heroin*, properly a trade-name, bestowed, one feels, somewhat arbitrarily in reference to Latin *heroïcus*, Greek *hērōikos*, of a hero.

Chloroform merely adapts French *chloroforme*, a compound of *chloro-*, the combining form of *chlorine* (from Greek *khloros*, greenish-yellow or pale-green), and *formyl* (*form*ic acid+the chemical suffix *-yl*); *ether*, as an anaesthetic, drastically specializes *ether*, air, the atmosphere, earlier the clear sky, earliest the heavens, and derives from Old French *ethere* (modern *éther*), from Latin *aether*, from Greek *aithēr*; *gas*, formerly much quoted as a word made from nothing, first appears, 1670, in a French translation of a work by the Flemish doctor and chemist, Jan van Helmont (1577–1644), who in the original says *Halitum illud gas vocavi, non longe a chao veterum*, 'I have called this exhalation *gas*, not far removed from the *chaos* of the Ancients': Latin *chaos*, from Greek *khaos*, a gaping, empty space.

All those drugs and anaesthetics take their names from Greek. But *penicillin* (chemical suffix *-in*, var. *-ine*) comes from Scientific Latin *Penicill*ium, a genus of fungi; *Penicillium* (chemical suffix *-ium*) comes from Latin *penicill*us, an artist's paint-brush, the diminutive of *penis* in its sense 'tail', the fungi being collectively named *Penicillium* from the tufts at the ends of their erect branchlets.

And how better end one's medical troubles than with *penicillin*?

FEVERISH ORIGINS

As perhaps one might expect, the names of fevers possess many different origins and etymologies; several fevers own more than one name; several names fall into more than one class; certain diseases called fevers are, strictly, not fevers at all—or, at least, not human fevers. To make matters worse, the author of this article has no medicine whatsoever. To offset that disadvantage, he does claim one great advantage: in 1915 he came off Gallipoli with paratyphoid and in 1918 he came off the Western Front with trench fever.

Fever and its medical synonym *pyrexia* are notable words. *Fever* derives, through Middle English *fevre* and earlier *fefre*, from Old English *fēfor* or *fēfer*, itself from Latin *febris*; the anterior history of the Latin word is tantalizingly obscure, but its adjective *febrilis* accounts for *febrile*. *Pyrexia* is a modern Scientific Latin coinage from the Greek *puressein*, to be feverish, from *puretos*, a fever, originally a fiery or burning heat, from *pur*, a fire, which has many Indo-European cognates, especially the German *Feuer* and the English *fire*—but not, oddly enough, the French *feu*, which represents L *focus*, a hearth, a fireplace.

Before we pass to the names of specific fevers, it is worth noting that *Texas fever* is a cattle disease and that *African Coast fever, East Coast Fever, Rhodesian fever*, are unscientific terms for piroplasmosis or babesiasis, likewise occurring among domesticated quadrupeds.

The names of human fevers may, for their origins, be divided—most unmethodically, I fear, yet not unreasonably, I hope—into:

physiological and other scientific;
geographical;
African and Asiatic (other than geographical);
colour and other popular names;
jessor.

Of the physiological and other scientific names, the following are selected for their general interest: *biliary, puerperal, rheumatic; enteric, typhus, typhoid*. A *biliary* fever, obviously, is connected with the bile; it comes from the French adjective *biliaire*, from L *bīlis*, the bile, a word that, despite its Celtic cognates, has an obscure earlier history. *Puerperal* fever, caused by and supervening upon childbirth, derives from L *puerpera*, a woman lying-in: *puer*, a child +*parere*, to bear one. Basically, *puer* is a young growing creature. It has very numerous Indo-European cognates, with, I suspect, the synonymous Gr *pais* among them. A *rheumatic* fever, commonest among children and young people, is characterized by acute rheumatic pains; and *rheumatic* comes, via French and Latin, from Gr *rheumatikos*, the adjective of *rheuma*, which, again via Latin and French, yields the archaic *rheum*, a watery discharge from nose and eyes, hence a cold: Gr *rheuma* is intimately related to *rhein*, to flow, and therefore ultimately related to our *stream*—compare 'streaming eyes'.

Enteric, short for *enteric fever*, now called *typhoid fever*, descends from the Gr *enterikos*, adjective of *enteron*, an intestine, itself a development from *en*, in, into, precisely as L *intestinus* is a development from the synonymous L *in*. The name *typhoid* (*fever*) was probably suggested by Gr *tuphōdēs*, delirious with fever; *typhoid* was originally the adj. of *typhus*, now a differentiated disease; *typhus* is a Scientific Latin form-and-sense adaptation of Gr *tuphos*, smoke, hence the stupor arising from fever; and Gr *tuphos* is akin to L *fumus*, smoke, hence both to English *fume* and, by folk-etymology, to English *typhoon*, which, every schoolboy knows (as, near enough, Macaulay used to remark whenever he wished to 'pull a particularly fast one'), has travelled all the way from Canton, where the original possessed the approximate form *tai-fung*.

Geographical names of fevers include *African fever* or dengue; *Hawaiian fever*; *Hughli fever*, severe, malarial, confined to Bengal and named from the Hughli river; *West African*, or blackwater, *fever*; *Panama*, usually called *Chagres*, *fever*, from the Central American river Chagres, which forms part of the Panama Canal; *Queensland fever*, first described in that State, but occurring also in, e.g., North America; *Rocky Mountain spotted fever*, tick-borne, once thought peculiar to that region but now known to occur elsewhere in the United States; *Roman fever*, that severe form of malaria which afflicts Rome and its neighbourhood—or formerly did so; *Salonika*, or trench, *fever*, far from being confined, during the war of 1914–18, to the region of Salonika in north-eastern Greece.

Of the non-geographical and non-chromatic Asiatic and African fever-names, two demand a particular mention: *jungle fever* and *dengue*. The former, a dangerous form of malaria, occurs in the jungles of the East Indies. *Jungle* anglicizes the Hindustani and Mahratti *jangal*, waste land, hence, waste land covered with trees, hence a forest; the native word comes from Sanskrit *jangala*, waste land, wilderness, desert, but its earlier history is unknown. From Hindustani it passed into Persian, then into the English of travellers; but its modern general European, including English, currency arose from the widespread Anglo-Indian and Franco-Indian use of the word in the eighteenth century. *Dengue*, on the other hand, represents a West Indian Spanish folk-etymological alteration—after Spanish *dengue*, affectation or prudery—of 'ki*dinga*popo', the Swahili name of this fever; related African dialects exhibit forms and senses either identical or easily recognizable. Also from the Swahili term comes, again by folk-etymology, the English *dandy* or *dandy fever*. *Dengue* has other non-scientific names, such as *African fever*, *breakbone fever*, *red fever*, all of which indicate certain characteristics of the disease.

Some of the fevers already mentioned bear what are clearly popular names. Perhaps the most representative group of such names consists of those which indicate a symptomatic colour. To a layman, the most sinister of these is the malarial *blackwater fever*, referring to the bloody urine. Then there are the *yellow*, from the presence of jaundice—the *purple*—the *scarlet*, now also *scarlatina*, a Scientific Latin elaboration consisting of *scarlet*, plus the suffix *-ina*—and *black fever*, a synonym of *Rocky Mountain spotted fever*.

Etymologically more interesting, however, are the other popular names, of which the following are probably the best

known: *strangers' fever, spotted fever, hay fever, trench fever, malaria.*
Spotted fever is mostly applied either to typhus or to various
diseases having a rickets characteristic; *strangers' fever,* to any
local fever easily acquired by newcomers. Strictly, *hay fever* is
caused by pollen inhaled from various plants. *Trench fever* or, as
the doctors of 1914–18 called it, *pyrexia of unknown origin,* or, just
to make it even more difficult for an ignorant soldier, *P.U.O.,*
resulted from the unhygienic conditions of trench warfare. But
one did not have to be occupying trenches to catch it, nor, as
most of the medical and other dictionaries so cheerfully assure
us, was it always mild; also it is no less a recurrent disease than,
say, malaria. *Malaria,* adopted from Italian, forms a specialized
sense of *mal'aria,* i.e. *mala aria,* bad air, and was so named
because of the belief that the disease came from noxious
exhalations of the Central Italian marshes (hence *paludal,* or
marsh, fever), especially those in the neighbourhood of Rome
(hence *Roman fever*); the real culprit escaped detection until
1899. Apparently the earliest mention in English is Horace
Walpole's 'a horrid thing called the mal'aria' in a letter of
1740.

Popular names for typhus are numerous, but mostly archaic;
all indicate either the place of origin or the circumstances of the
disease; *ship fever, prison fever, camp fever;* and *war fever, famine
fever.* These designations are now rare because hygiene, whether
civilian or military, has been so much improved. Compare the
obsolescent *cesspool fever* or typhoid.

But the name that perplexed me the longest (all of fifteen
minutes) was *jessor fever,* as, with small *j,* not capital *J,* it is
printed in *Dorland's Medical Dictionary,* which defines the term
as 'a long-standing intermittent fever common in parts of India'.
After consulting both the few medical dictionaries and all the
British, American, Continental encyclopaedias familiar to me—
works that do at least include the World Health Organization's
official classification of diseases and the magnificent *Enciclopedia
Italiana*—and receiving an intolerably dusty answer, I beat my
head in disgust and muttered, 'You idiot, *jessor* is probably
geographical', and from a remote youth undistinguished for
geographical knowledge, dredged the place-name *Jessore.* With

head bowed in shame, I tottered to the open shelves of the
British Museum library, took out that splendid gazetteer, the
Columbia, and read this illuminating passage: '*Jessore* . . .
district . . . in Ganges Delta . . . Alluvial plain . . . Extensive
marshes . . . largely responsible for high malarial mortality.'
The *Columbia* added that Jessore was 'formerly called Yaso-
hara', information which miraculously salved the self-esteem
that had been so deeply perforated by a failure to perceive,
immediately perceive, that here was yet another instance of
Name into Word.

THE LANGUAGE OF WITCHCRAFT
AND MAGIC

MACBETH: . . . *You secret, black, and midnight hags,*
What is't you do?
THE WITCHES: *A deed without a name.*

EVER since the beginning of recorded history, and, doubtless for thousands of years before that, magic and witchcraft and diabolism have existed as a dark, seemingly imperishable thread—an ugly streak—in and against the brighter stuff of an undeniable progress towards civilization. We know of the Witch of Endor; but, far more anciently, Egypt, the Mesopotamian basin and China had had their magic. We know of the witches of Salem; but between Endor and Salem lay some 2700 years and as many dark pages. After Salem, witchcraft apparently decreased, but evil possession continued to reach its apex in the maniacal possession of a Hitler; and lives there a man so rash, a woman so foolish, as to say, or at any rate to believe, that Satanism or magic or even witchcraft has disappeared?

Magic in general, witchcraft in particular, and diabolism: these form the three main branches of a vast subject; and although magic, witchcraft, diabolism do not, in themselves, concern me here, yet they afford a very convenient division of a few of the more important terms:

I: *magic, magical, magician, enchanting, black magic* and *white magic; enchantment, enchanter* and *enchantress; sorcery—sorcerous— sorcerer* and *sorceress.* (The generally accepted names for the four types of magical practice are: *Sympathetic magic; divination; thaumaturgy; incantation.* To these terms, we should, for completeness, add: *divinery, thaumaturgic* and *thaumaturge, incantatory,* and that particular kind of *divination* which we call *necromancy,* and *necromancer.*)

II: *Witchcraft* and *wizardry, witching, bewitching . . . wizardly, witch* and *wizard; sabbath* or *sabbat; Walpurgisnacht; coven; cast a spell.*

III. *Possession; demon and familiar;* the *Devil* or *Satan; diabolical, Satanic, diabolism, diablerie, Satanism; black Mass; Mephistopheles* and *pact with the Devil.*

Ancient Persia and Media had a priestly caste, the *Magi,* who enjoined that the deities of evil must, no less than the deities of good, be worshipped. These Median Magoi as the Greeks called them, were the very masters of knowledge. Therefore, in a primitive society, they interpreted dreams and practised necromancy: hence *magos,* a sorcerer, a magician: hence *magikos,* transliterated into Latin as *magicus;* hence the old French adjective *magique:* hence the English adjective *magic* (often elaborated into *magical*). Greeks spoke of *magikē* tekhnē, magic art, and soon shortened it to *magikē,* which became Latin *magice,* which naturally became the French noun *magique,* which duly became the English noun *magic.* The Latin for a sorcerer was *magicus,* which French converted into *magicien,* which English adapted as *magician.* To medieval ecclesiastics, *magic* was, on the one hand, natural or *white* and therefore comparatively innocuous (indeed, modern science owes much to it) and, on the other hand, unnatural (sorcery and witchcraft) or *black* and therefore dangerous, evil, forbidden.

Sorcery, the use of such power as can be gained either by controlling evil spirits, or, at the least, by enlisting their assistance, derives from Middle English *sorcerie,* adopted from Old French, which had formed it from *sorcier* (whence, by the way, the English *sorcerer*), a sorcerer, from a probable Low Latin *sortiarius,* itself from Latin *sors* (genitive *sortis*), a decision by lot, the lot appointed for each of us, hence fate. And, on the stem *sorcer-,* English built the adjective *sorcerous.*

Formerly, the employment of magic, or of sorcery, was called *enchantment;* nor has this sense of the word entirely disappeared. To subject someone to magic was to *enchant* him; the person doing this was the *enchanter* or, maybe, the *enchantress;* an *enchanting* person could be very dangerous. (She still is.) The effective base of all these words rests upon the Old French *enchanter*, from Latin *incantare*. With the latter we shall meet again at *incantation*.

Of the already mentioned four types of magical practice, *sympathetic magic* is so named because like is supposed, not only to *affect*, but even to *effect*, like; certain results, therefore can be obtained by mimicry or by the inclusion of names in a spell. Compare the *sympathetic powder* of the medieval alchemists: a powder so efficacious that it healed a wounded man by merely being applied to the blood flowing from the wound or even to the sword that inflicted it.

Divination—adjective *divinational*; archaic verb, to *divine*; agent *diviner* or *divineress*—consists, in this context, of the discovery of hidden knowledge, especially of the future, and the word comes from medieval Latin *divinatio* (classical Latin *diuinatio*), oblique stem *divination-*; *divinatio* was formed from *divinus* (classical *diuinus*), itself from *deus*, a god; *deus* basically means 'he who illuminates, (hence) reveals' and is akin to *dies*, the luminous part of a day, hence a day.

Thaumaturgy, literally '*wonder-working*', includes legerdemain and jugglery and the trickery exercised by or through evil spirits; it tends to imply magic of a dubious kind. The word derives from Greek *thaumatourgia*: compare *thaumatourgos*, wonder-working or -worker, a compound of *thaumat*, oblique stem of *thauma*, a wonder, a miracle+ —*o*—, connective element+*ergos*, working or worker (*ergon*, work). The agent is a *thaumaturge*, from Medieval Latin *thaumaturgus*, from Greek *thaumatourgos*; the adjective is *thaumaturgic*.

Necromancy is divination effected by communication with the dead: the Greek *nekromanteia* joins *nekro*, combining form of *nekros*, a corpse, to *manteia*, prophecy, divination, from *mantis*, a diviner or seer. The Greek term passed through Latin *necromantia* on its way to English. Middle English *nigromancie*, like Old French *nigromance*, reflects the influence of folk-etymology, there being a confusion with Latin *niger*, black; that confusion accounts for an old synonym: *the black art*.

Incantation refers to the ritualistic aspect of magic—the recital of formulas and spells. The word comes through French from Late Latin *incantatio*, oblique stem *incantation*, from *incantare*, to recite a spell over someone; *incantare* is a compound of *in*, into, directed at, and *cantare*, to chant, to sing; the rare Latin agent *incantator* (hence the adjective *incantatory*) has been superseded by the French-dressed *enchanter*.

We now reach witchcraft and the less usual wizardry. The agent *wizard*, immediate origin of adjective *wizardly* and of *wizardry*, derives from Middle English *wysards*: *wys*, wise, and *-ard*, a suffix denoting a person—often an unfavourable suffix, as in *coward* and *bastard*. *Witchcraft* simply means the *craft* (Old English *craeft*, skill or cunning) of a witch, originally a man or a woman practising magic, divination, necromancy and so forth, but finally, and throughout modern English, applied to a woman practitioner. *Witch* derives from Middle English *wicche*, which thus merges Old English *wicce*, a female, and *wicca*, a male witch. From the noun comes the verb 'to *witch*', with adjective *witching* or, in a strengthened form, *bewitching*, now rarely applied in their original, strong senses. *Witchery*, originally the practice of witchcraft, now connotes the charm, indeed the fascination, exercised by some women over some men. With the decline of *witching, bewitching, witchery*, compare that of *wizard* used as an adjective.

An assembly of witches is a *coven*, the usual form, or *covin*, sometimes spelt *covine*: from Old French *covin* or *covine*, a variation of *covent*, a gathering, literally a coming-together: *covent*, like English *convent*, descends from Latin *conventus*, an assembly, a meeting, a coming-together; the medieval Latin *conventus* means also a convent, a residence for those who, in religion, have come together. Like 'to *convene*', *convent* and *covent*, hence *coven* and *covin*, derive from Latin *convenire*, to meet together, to gather, to assemble: *con-* or *co-*, with, together+*venire* (classical Latin *uenire*), to come.

A midnight assembly of witches and sorcerers, but also of demons, meeting to celebrate their orgies, is called a *sabbath* or, as in French, a *sabbat*. English *sabbath* comes from Middle English *sabath*, earlier *sabat*, which derives from Latin *sabbatum*, a transliteration of Greek *sabbaton*, an adaptation of Hebrew *shabbath*, day of rest, itself from *shabath*, to rest: from rest to holiday to festivity to orgiastic festivity forms an easy transitional chain of sense, a chain exemplifying a world-old, world-wide, never-ceasing process of thought and language. One particular witches' sabbath has become famous: that which, according to German folklore, was held on the Brocken, one of the Harz mountains, on the eve of the feast-day of St Walburga or Walpurgis: *Walpurgisnacht* (German *Nacht*, night) or, in its anglicized form, *Walpurgis Night*.

Like the magicians and sorcerers, the witches and wizards were skilled in the casting of spells. To *cast a spell* is to chant or recite a magic formula or word over someone, in order to dominate or control or incapacitate him; the victim of such *spell-binding* became *spell-bound*. *Spell* has derived, unchanged, from Old English, is akin to other words in Old Teutonic languages, and occurs also in *gospel*, Old English *god-spell*, good news, *spell* being originally nothing more sinister than a 'spoken word'.

Linking magic, sorcery, witchcraft to an even more potent, far-reaching and dangerous power is *possession*. Possession by an evil spirit; above all, possession either by one of the Devil's emissaries or by the Devil himself. *Possession*, like *the possessed*, comes, for all practical purposes, from Latin *possidere*, to possess, be in possession of, a fusion of *potis*, able, capable, and *sedēre*, to sit: to sit in power: hence, to sit in power over. A person *possessed* is one who is dominated by an external power or an extraneous personality, especially a demon. A *demon* may be either master or servant; as in the latter, acting maleficently, he is sometimes called a *familiar*, short for *familiar spirit*, which, in the beneficent sense, is an attendant and protective spirit, like the Greek *daimon*. Now *daimon*, strictly any divinity, became Latin *daemon*, which soon acquired the sense 'a spirit', especially 'an evil spirit'; and *daemon* became the French *démon* and, perhaps through French, the English *demon*, originally a divinity or deity regarded less as a person than as a supernatural power, but soon an evil spirit, a devil; the adjective *demoniac* denotes either 'devilish' or 'possessed by a devil'.

The most perilous, powerful and pervasive of all demons or

devils is *the Devil*, known also by a score of other names (for instance, the *Adversary*: mankind's greatest foe) but by none more impressive than *Satan*.

Devil, which sounds so very English, descends from Old English *dēofol* or *dēoful*: it has, therefore, been English a very long time. *Dēoful*, however, comes from Late Latin *diabolus*. That may seem a very far cry; yet compare *debble* or *debbil*, dialectal and Negro versions of *devil*. *Diabolus* merely transliterates the Greek *diabolos*, a devil (originally) a slanderer, from *diaballein*, to slander, originally to throw (*ballein*) across (*dia*). The adjective is *diabolic* from Greek *diabolikos*; the practices, the machinations, the wiles of a devil, notably of *the* Devil, constitute *diabolism*, formed from *diabol-* and the *-ism* of 'the isms'. Diabolism is occasionally known by its French name, *Diablerie*—a word consisting of *diable*, a devil, and the *-erie* we find in *Jacquerie* and in English *mystery*; *-erie* or *ery*, ultimately from Greek, connotes 'activity in' or 'professional work at'.

Diabolism, however, usually goes by the name of *Satanism*, which, like *Satanic*, comes direct from *Satan*. This *Satan* has been adopted from late Latin, the Latin of the early Christian Church, which adopted it from Greek, which adopted—rather, adapted it—from Hebrew. In Hebrew, the word designates an adversary. *Satan* is much to be preferred to such poetic euphemisms as *the Prince of Darkness* and to such hieratic pomposities as *the Arch-fiend*.

The power and the dignity of Satan have overcome the *louche* pettiness of that supremely crude travesty, the *black Mass*; have overcome the fantasy of many a *pact with the Devil*; have overcome the ridicule brought upon him by such clumsy associates as Beelzebub and by such theatrical imitators as Mephistopheles. After an eclipse lasting throughout most of the eighteenth and nineteenth centuries, Satan has returned to European literature; by (say) 1900, he had been laughed out of existence. He remained 'an exploded myth' until the war of 1914–18, when people began to doubt their doubts. The war of 1939–45 virtually reinstated him. Two such world-scarring, soul-blasting wars are perhaps attributable only to one of two forces: either to Satan or to an incredible stupidity in mankind;

or, of course, to that stupidity employed by Satan as an invincible weapon. The Catholic Church has, I'm told, never ceased to warn its members against the formidable patience and the well-nigh infinite resourcefulness of Satan the Great Adversary. It is, therefore, natural that it should be the Catholic novelists of France (for instance, Mauriac) and Britain (Graham Greene) who have put Satan back, not on a pedestal, but where he can be seen and watched. For, as that macabre poseur but true poet, Baudelaire, said:

The Devil's best trick is to persuade us that he does not exist.

THE LANGUAGE OF THE MYSTICS

Mysticism. The doctrine or belief that direct knowledge of God, of spiritual truth, of ultimate reality, etc., is attainable through immediate intuition, insight, or illumination, and in a way differing from ordinary sense perception or ratiocination. Any type of theory asserting the possibility of attaining knowledge or power through faith or spiritual insight.—*Webster's New International Dictionary.*

Mysticism means union with God, that is to say with a Being conceived as the supreme and ultimate reality.—W. R. Inge, *Mysticism in Religion,* 1947.

MYSTICISM, in its purest and severest form, has been negatively described by the Very Reverend Dean W. R. Inge, often and misleadingly called 'The Gloomy Dean'. 'I cannot,' he says, 'accept any definition which identifies mysticism with excited or hysterical emotionalism, with sublimated eroticism, with visions and revelations, with supernatural (dualistically opposed to natural) activities, nor, on the philosophical side, with irrationalism.' That would rule out St Teresa, many Indian mystics, and others; spiritual ecstasy need not be hysterical, nor visions the mark of a disordered imagination.

'The literature of the subject' is vast; that dealing critically with the subject is large. The following works present most aspects of Western and, by implication, many of the principal aspects of Eastern mysticism:

William James: *The Varieties of Religious Experience,* 1902. Still the best book on the subject he treats.

R. Pettazzoni: *I Misteri,* 1926. Historically a very important work, dealing with the ancient mysteries of Egypt, Asia Minor, Greece, India.

Evelyn Underhill: *Mysticism,* 1911; many editions, some of them extensively revised, have since appeared.

W. R. Inge: *Mysticism in Religion,* 1947.

An excellent account of the British contribution is that in

Gerald Bullett's *The English Mystics*, 1950. Like Dean Inge, Mr Bullett speaks with affection and admiration of the anonymous fourteenth century author of *The Cloud of Unknowing*, sympathetically edited by Evelyn Underhill in 1922. Among American writers, one draws especial attention to J. B. Pratt's *The Religious Consciousness*, J. H. Leuba's *The Psychology of Religious Mysticism* and Josiah Royce's works, *passim*. Mysticism, whether Occidental or Oriental, has more engaged the scrutiny of American than of British philosophers.

Having postulated that mysticism constitutes not only a philosophy and a religion but also a way of life, and having noted that *yoga*, whether spiritual or practical, forms a very important kind of mysticism, I pass to my true subject, the language of mysticism. It is merely prudent to exclude the technicalities and to confine the examination to the terms known to all those who have a smattering of the subject and even to the ordinary intelligent and cultured reader.

These terms fall into three groups, representative only, not exhaustive. The general terms I propose to treat are: *mystery* and *mysticism*; *mystic* (or *mystical*) *union—attainment—absolute*; *initiate (initiation)* and *adept*; *gnosis*; *contemplation* and *meditation*; *ecstasy* and *rapture*. The Western I shall restrict to three: *Plotinism, Rosicrucianism, quietism*. The Eastern to *yoga* and *yogi*; *atman*; *karma*; *maya*; and *nirvana*. Intimately linked with, and forming the key to, both Eastern and Western mysticism: *the way*.

All the ancient *mysteries* or secret cults contained *mystic* ideas either germinal or matured; and to all, admission could be obtained only by a ceremonial initiation. Full participants were *initiates*; special initiates were *adepts*. In short, mysticism has derived from the ancient Egyptian, Phrygian, Hindu and Greek (hence, the Latin) mysteries.

Mystery, like the French *mystère*, comes from Latin *mysterium*, itself from Greek *mustērion*, originally meaning a secret thing or act, hence a secret ceremony, hence a secret cult. If we examine *mustērion*, we find that *-ērion*, whence Latin *-erium*, whence English *-ery*, is a suffix, connoting 'a matter of, an example of,' as in, say, *sorcery* or *jugglery*. The first, the important, the fundamental element, therefore, is *must-*, which appears also in *mustikos* (Latin *mysticus*, English *mystic*, adjective then also noun), the adjective of *mustēs*, a close-mouthed person, hence one who has been initiated into a mystery. *Mustēs* has the suffix *-istēs*, which after a vowel is usually shortened to *-stēs*; and *-(i)stēs* connotes 'one who does, or is, something'. The basic element of *mustēs* is therefore *mu-*, which, we notice, constitutes the stem of *muein*, to be closed, a verb applied to the eyes and especially to the lips: hence, to be close-mouthed. That stem *mu-* represents a basic idea and a fundamental sound: *mu* or, in English, *moo*, as in the child's *moo-cow*. Now, *muein*, (of lips, eyes) to be closed or shut, has 1st Person Singular *muō*. This *muō* is intransitive: to which the transitive complement is *mueō*, with infinitive *muein*, to close or shut; a specialized sense of the transitive *mueō* is 'I initiate (someone) into a mystery'—by 'closing his mouth', so that he will not speak of the mysteries.

As one has to be trained for and in a mystery, so one has to be trained for and in mysticism. The mystic's *mystic attainment* is accomplished when he has achieved *mystic union* with the *Mystic Absolute* or the Ultimate and Absolute Reality or God. The third term, however, is used also in the form *mystic absolute*, which bears several shades of meaning, the most relevant being 'the mystic's interpretation of the organic unity of all reality'— a reality essentially spiritual.

Initiation (Latin *initiatio*, genitive *initiationis*) derives from *initiat-*, the base of *initiatus* (whence 'an *initiate*' and 'to *initiate*') —the past participle of *initiare*, to begin something, hence to begin (someone) in (something)—itself from *inititium*, a beginning, but originally a going-in, from *inire*, to go in, to go into (*in* prefixed to *ire*, to go). An *adept* derives his name from *adeptus*, having obtained: elliptical for *adeptus artem*, having obtained (the mastery of) an art, here the art of the mystery itself, hence of the mysticism involved. *Adept* is very closely connected with *apt*.

The positive knowledge, the *gnosis*, of philosophy becomes the *gnosis*, or secret knowledge, of mystics, who apply the term to a knowledge either of spiritual truth or of matters commonly thought to be apprehensible by faith alone. The word has come, through Latin, from Greek *gnōsis*, a derivative of *gignōskein*, to know. *Gignōskein* falls into three parts: *gi-* and *gnōsk-* and *-ein*, of which the third indicates the infinitive, and the first reduplicates the *gnō-* of *gnōsk-*. With the central element, *gnōsk-*, compare *nōsc-*, the stem of Latin *nōscere*, to know. Both the Latin *nōsc-* and the Greek *gnōsk-* are elaborations of *nō-*, earlier *gnō-* (*gnōscere* is attested in very ancient Latin); and *gnō-* corresponds to the *knō-* of English 'to *know*'.

Contemplation, a sustained perception and awareness of God, and *meditation*, a profound, sustained reflection upon a religious subject, come from *contemplation-* and *meditation-*, the oblique stems of Latin *contemplatio, meditatio*, the latter meaning literally a measuring and the former literally a being-seen from every point simultaneously (*con*, with, together)—as was the well-sited *templum* or temple. The priests usually ensured that their temples should be well placed.

Rapture, a carrying away (Latin *rapere*, to seize, to abduct), hence a being carried away, hence an emotional or a spiritual transport, is less used by mystics than *ecstasy*, which, through Old French *extasie* (compare the variant English spelling *extasy*) and Late Latin *ecstasis*, comes from Greek *ekstasis*, a setting (something) out of place: *ek*, out, and *stasis*, a placing, literally a standing, from *histanai*, to set, literally to stand; the basic element is *stan-*, akin to English *stand* and Latin *stare*, present participle *stans*, genitive *stantis* (oblique stem, *stant-*). Ecstasy is not to be confused with *illumination*, enlightenment— that stage along the mystic way at which the believer's soul attains to an understanding of spiritual things. *Illumination* stems back to Latin *lux*, light.

I have selected, as the Western terms, the names of three important varieties of mysticism: *Plotinism, Rosicrucianism, quietism. Plotinism* is the *-ism* or philosophy of *Plotinus* (A.D. 205–270), keenest mind in all the Alexandrian school of Neo-platonists. Plato himself, by the way, had been something of a mystic. The name *Plotinus* is the Latin shape of the Greek *Ploutinos*, which represents an *-inos* derivative, connoting 'of, like, descended from', of *Ploutos*, Latin and English *Plutus*, a personification—compare the *Dives* of the New Testament—of *ploutos*, wealth, itself akin to *plousios* or *ploutios*, rich, both deriving from *polus*, numerous, *polu*, much: he who has many sheep, much property, is rich.

Rosicrucianism derives from *Rosicrucian*, which refers to Christian *Rosenkreuz*—by monks called Frater *Rosae Crucis*, Brother 'of the Rosy Cross'—founder, in fifteenth-century Germany, of a philosophico-religious secret society. *Quietism* arose in Spain, its principles having been set forth in Miguel de Molinos's *The Spiritual Guide*, 1675: for this doctrine of spiritual self-annihilation, its author went to, remained and even died in prison. Modern quietism is a far less extreme doctrine.

The Eastern terms are more important: *yoga, atman, karma, maya, nirvana*. *Yoga*, akin to Latin *iugum*, Greek *zugon*, a yoke, means 'union'; specifically, with God. The Sanskrit *yoga*, stem *yog-*, has a derivative, *yogin* (stem *yog-*), which became Hindi *yogi*, adopted by the West for a follower of the philosophy of yoga or a practiser of the yoga system of mental discipline. Yoga, as practised, not merely discussed, entails certain physical exercises, such as the holding of a posture and the control of one's breathing. A different breath is implied in the mystic *atman*: Sanskrit *ātman*, literally a breathing, a breath, hence breath in general, became the breather's self, hence his soul, hence the Universal Self or Supreme Spirit: compare semantically (that is, for the idea) the Latin *spiritus*, a breathing, a breath, and finally, in Church Latin, *spiritus*, the Spirit (the Holy Spirit). With the Sanskrit word *ātman* itself, compare the Greek *atmos*, vapour: and vapour is what you see when you strongly exhale.

Much better known to the non-mystic is *karma*, adopted likewise from Sanskrit. Strictly a Buddhist technicality, *karma*, literally an act or action in general, hence fate regarded as the necessary result of the sum of one's actions, tends in mysticism to denote the ever-continuing and subtly accumulating work and working-out of every act and thought and wish and emotion, especially if it be a controlled or, at the least, directed working-out. Another well-known, though again rather vaguely apprehended, term is *nirvana*, popularly understood to mean

oblivion to care and pain and thought to have some odd connexion with narcotics. In Buddhism, *nirvana* signifies extinction,
in the human heart, of hatred, passion, delusion, and—an
aspect important for mysticism—a consequent spiritual condition of supreme beatitude, free, however, of complacency.
The literal meaning of Sanskrit *nirvana* is: extinction, as the
blowing-out of a flame; it derives from *nirva*, to blow. *Maya*,
from Sanskrit *maya*, illusion, akin to Greek *mimos*, Latin *mimus*,
a mime, a theatrical illusion, has various meanings in Buddhism
and in mysticism: they range from God's power of manifestation and creation to man's power, as it were magical, of
creation.

In all ethical systems, in all philosophies, in all religions,
there is *the way*: the way to life eternal; the way to communion
with God; the way to the good life, here and now, here and
until one dies: to the Christian, it usually signifies the Christian
religion (compare the *hodos* of the Greek New Testament); to
the educated Chinese it might well recall Lao Tse's *The Way*,
or *The Path, to Virtue* (sixth century B.C.); to the mystic, it
denotes either of two complementary ways—the inward way,
that of introspection; or the path trodden, the highroad won,
by the unitive, or unifying, vision. Of the innumerable metaphors employed by the world's religions, this is one of the three
or four most ancient; it is more than natural, it is inevitable;
it is also one of the most heartening. Mankind, travelling it
knows not whither, has a constant, less easily wearied com-
panion: the human spirit, journeying along a path it may not
always discern very clearly yet continues to tread, hopefully
and valiantly.

PARANOIACS AND PSYCHOLEPTS

The Language of Psychiatry

'People's subconscious selves were emerging, which is always disturbing
and sometimes catastrophic.'

Claude Houghton, *The Enigma of Conrad Stone*, 1952.

A STUDY of the language of psychiatry would require a
monograph. Some say that it deserves one. But here we are
concerned only with a certain number of such terms as have
already crept or swept their way, or seem about to do so, into
the speech of the merely educated and cultured: that invaluable, often stupidly derided, 'general intelligent public'
which does far more than the cliques and the coteries, the highbrows and the hysterics, to maintain both civilization itself
and such fosterers of civilization as painters and sculptors,
musicians and composers, poets and dramatists and other
writers.

Psychiatry was taken over by novelists and biographers long
before it reached the cinema. The cinema never plunges
bravely: long after its seniors, it enters the water, only to paddle
timidly: but then, the cinema tries to serve, not 'the general
intelligent public' but merely 'the general public'. I must,
however, admit that I heard at a cinema before I read in fiction
'the blessèd word' *psychosomatic*, applied to those disabilities of
the body (Greek *sōma*) which have been caused by the mind.

In biography the result has often been unhappy; in the novel,
occasionally. The psychiatric novel was inaugurated by a
Canadian, C. Daly King, author of *The Psychology of Consciousness* (1932), in his three 'Obelists' novels, 1932–35, and in
several others during the later nineteen-thirties. He was succeeded in Britain by Nigel Balchin, whose first notable work in
the genre, *Mine Own Executioner*, appeared in 1945, and in the
United States by such a writer as Joseph Franklin Bardin (*The*

Deadly Percheron, 1946). Perhaps even more significant in the invasion of English by psychiatry is the use of psycho-analytic terms by novelists not primarily concerned with psychiatry at all: for instance, by 'Edmund Crispin', from 1944 onwards, in Britain, and by Herbert Brean, since 1948, in America. To commit the cardinal sin of quoting oneself ('So very egocentric, darling!'): 'The methods of Freud have been experimented with: accelerated for speed-lovers, modified for the squeamish, and simplified for those readers who prefer the reach-me-downs of the circulating-library shelves. The result is—the better the psychiatry, the worse the novel. . . . The genre of the psychiatric novel has yet to evolve a satisfactory *modus operandi*' (*British and American English since 1900*, with John W. Clark).

After that shamelessly inadequate note on psychiatry in literature, I hasten to the subject proper: some of the psychiatric terms known to and even used by the well-informed layman.

The senses of these terms are constantly shifting. I make no attempt to nail down the latest nuances; in a year's, at most two years' time, those nuances will perhaps be dead. But several generalities have to be considered before we can safely deal with psychiatric terms proper. *Psychology*, the science of the mind, has, in its practical aspect, a modern development: *psychoanalysis*, usually restricted to Freud's method and to more recent modifications: in its medical aspect, psycho-analysis is called *psychiatry*.

Psychiatry is simply the English form of Modern Latin *psychiatria*, a compound of the Greek *psukhē*, mind, soul, and *iatreia*, healing, cure. *Psukhē*, usually and deceptively written *psychē*, became *psyche* in Latin. The *psyche*, variously defined as soul or spirit or mind, is best defined as spirit, provided that we understand the term to include emotion and impulse as well as mind, and soul as well as intellect and emotions.

'You'—any you whatsoever—'do not like to discover evidence of the unnatural extremes to which the human psyche can drive itself': Herbert Brean, *Hardly a Man Is Now Alive*, 1951.

The word *psyche* demands a closer examination. With an admirable terseness, *Webster's New International Dictionary*, in the great recension of 1934, states the etymology of *Psyche*, the Ancient Greek personification of the soul, to be 'Latin, from Greek *Psychē*, Psyche, from *psychē*, the soul' and then, at *psychic*, derives *psychē* from *psychein* (better *psukhein*), to breathe. The basic sense of *psukhē*, is a blowing, a breath, hence breath in general and breath as vital principle; without breath there is no life; life—in mankind, at least—is expressed in and by mind, emotions, spirit; breath therefore becomes equated to spirit. Compare, therefore, *spirit* itself, deriving from Latin *spiritus*, which in Late and especially in Church Latin means spirit and (*spiritus sanctus*) Holy Spirit, but in Classical Latin means, predominantly, breath of life or, as in earlier Latin, merely breath; in Classical and earlier Latin, the soul was denoted by either *anima* or *animus*, the former being slightly the more abstract. Both *spiritus* and *psukhē*, relating to the most important thing of all, very naturally tend to exist in their own rights: only with difficulty and complete uncertainty can either word be traced to an Indo-European stem. Much the same can be said of *breath*, which has far fewer and much less important ramifications.

Between terms peculiar to psychiatry itself and those belonging to the rather wider field of psycho-analysis, there exists a very convenient link: the pair of terms, *psychosis* and *neurosis*, which are, of course, common to both. Kept within the bounds of good, as opposed to common, sense, *psychosis* and *neurosis* are paramount terms; they are also sacred to Freudians and hieratic to psychiatrists, for many of whom they amount to shibboleths. Frequently confused by laymen, *psychosis* and *neurosis* mean respectively 'a mental process' (*psychology*) or 'mental disease, especially a derangement' (psychiatry) and, *neurosis*, 'an activity of the nervous system' (physiology and psychology) or 'a nervous disorder that, without apparent physical lesion, is functional' (psychiatry); neuroses are sometimes distinguished as *actual neurosis*, e.g. neurasthenia, and *psychoneurosis*, e.g. hysteria. The element *-osis*, deriving from Greek *-ōsis*, signifies a state or a condition, especially either a diseased or at the least a disordered, condition; and the determining part of *neurosis* is *neur-*, stem of Greek *neuron*, a nerve. One speaks of 'a *war* *psychosis*', 'a *fear psychosis*', or of 'an *anxiety neurosis*', 'a *compulsion neurosis*'. Even among the best psychiatrists, therefore, it is natural that these two words should sometimes overlap. We laymen are not always quite so stupid as we may seem to be. The adjectives, by the way, are *psychotic* and *neurotic*, both formed upon Greek models but not deriving from Greek words.

Psychiatric terms, used professionally and scrupulously by psychiatrists, are unexceptionable: a convenience, they comprise a jargon no more objectionable than the jargon—the technicalities—of doctors or engineers, a jargon with a status comparable with that of the learned professions and the skilled trades. The jargon of psychiatry becomes hateful only when it is employed to dazzle laymen; it becomes dangerous only in the mouths of unscrupulous practitioners and pretentious laymen.

The range of psychiatric terms is narrow, and their employment even by the medical profession has been general only since two or three years before World War I (1914–18); yet, perhaps because of the intangibles and imponderables involved, these terms, when used out of their proper sociological context, form perhaps the most fatuous and certainly one of the most snobbish of vocabularies.

Psychiatric terms fall, not unnaturally, into the two groups, General and Particular. This being a selective, not an exhaustive essay; in short, an essay, not a lexical study or paper; I am reducing the former group to *Freudian* and *Jungian—field— margin, marginal* and *periphery, peripheral—unconscious* and *subconscious—stimuli* and *reaction—subjective* and *objective*: and the latter group, the particularities, to *the ego* and *the id—introvert* and *extrovert—complex*, whether *inferiority* or *Oedipus—fixation— repression* and *frustration—inhibition* and *exhibitionism—depression* and *psycholepsy*—the various *phobias—narcissism—trauma—paranoia* and *schizophrenia—defence mechanism* and *escapism—compensation* and *sublimation—projection—wishful thinking* and *the death wish*—and, the ambition of laymen and psychiatrists alike, an *integrated personality*.

Sigmund Freud (1856–1939), that Austrian psychiatrist who dominated 'the Viennese School' and who based his theory and his practice upon a study of the unconscious and of the sexual impulses, has given us the adjective *Freudian*, especially in *the Freudian mechanisms*, dealing largely with the partly mental, partly instinctual compromises we all make between the promptings of the conscious and the insidiosities of the sub-conscious mind. Alfred Adler (1870–1937), another Austrian, belonged for some years to the Viennese group of psycho-analysts, but then seceded and developed his own pet theory: The desire to dominate is the most powerful of all desires. From him, *Adlerian*.

Carl Jung, however, is a Swiss psychiatrist, born in 1875; he too seceded. The *Jungian* system puts 'the vital impulse', the desire to live, in the first place: and as a general principle, Jung's is obviously far more fundamental than Adler's, rather more fundamental than Freud's: the instinct of self-preserva-tion in particular and the general, undefined wish to survive ('Life is sweet, brother, life is sweet': 'The most important thing in life is life') are, as every man (and woman) of good sense knows, constant, not intermittent. Jung is the best philosopher of the three: and psychiatrists of the 1960's will probably owe more to him than to Freud, most of whose jungle-ghosts have been laid or, at the lowest estimate, banished to the gibberers' garret where they belong.

Field: margin and *periphery*. One speaks of *the field of attention*, narrower than *the field of consciousness* or the entire range of objects of which one is conscious; the term has passed to psycho-logy from physics. On the *margin* or *periphery* of one's field of consciousness at any waking moment there lie a host of objects (including embryonic intimations, imprecise impulses, faint stirrings of fear) apprehended or felt only very vaguely and remotely: these objects, and the apprehension or the feeling, are said to be *marginal* or *peripheral*. In descriptions of the nervous system, physiologists and others speak of 'the peripheral termination of a nerve': hence the psychiatric application of the term. Etymologically, the basic sense of *margin* is 'edge', hence 'frontier'; and that of *periphery* is 'a carrying round', hence 'external boundary' (originally of a circle).

These marginal or peripheral matters link with *parapsychology*, etymologically 'the psychology of the beyond', and with *E.S.P.*

or *extra-sensory perceptions*, perceptive powers not easily explained by reference to the senses. Parapsychology, however, has so far been connected with psychiatry only remotely.

A pair of terms very closely associated with psychiatry is that of *unconscious* and *subconscious*, adjectives used as nouns. Roughly, one is *unconscious*, not conscious, when stunned, in a faint, or asleep; psycho-analysts use it both thus and in the restricted sense 'excluded, by repression, from consciousness'. Roughly, *subconscious*, under the conscious, less than the conscious, refers to those mental processes of which the *subject*, the agent or, in a different nuance, the patient, is unaware, as in 'a piece of subconscious reasoning'; *subconscious* is sometimes applied to emotions, as in 'He was impelled by a subconscious fear of being cheated'.

Subject, an agent, a patient, recalls the complementary *subjective*, predominantly or essentially personal, and *objective*, predominantly—for it can never be entirely—impersonal. Clearly, *subjective* and *objective* belong to all psychology.

More characteristically psychiatric is the phrase *react to stimuli* or *reactions to stimuli*. One responds to a *stimulus* as to a goad: Latin *stimulus*, a goad, originally physical, very soon also moral or emotional: a goad causes one to 'jump to it', to respond quickly. *Stimuli* are divided into *homologous* (Greek *homologos*, agreeing, being in agreement: *homos*, the same, compounded with *logos*, speech, reason, proportion) or *adequate*, and *heterologous* (Greek *heteros*, other, different, as in *heterodoxy*); strictly, this differentiation applies only to stimuli affecting the nervous system.

Thus we come to a few terms either mainly or, as for most of them, solely psychiatric. Of this selected group, only two— *psycholepsy* and *Electra complex*—have failed to penetrate the vocabulary of laymen; yet even they have reached the more erudite critics.

'His ego suffered', 'He wanted to boost my ego' and similar statements exemplify the popular use of *ego*. *Egocentric* has, in semi-popular use, been tending to supersede both *egoistic* and *egotistic*; in psychology, *egocentric* means, approximately, self-centred. Psychology equates 'the *ego*' to 'the self'; psychoanalysis confines it to mankind's self-preserving, hence also its self-assertive, tendency and thus differentiates it from *libido* (adjective: *libidinal*, not *libidinous*), mankind's primary motive or driving force, whether derived from the sexual impulse, as Freud maintained, or from the desire to survive, as Jung held. Behind ego and libido stands the *id*, that mass of fundamental tendencies from which spring the tendencies the psychiatrists call *ego* and *libido*. This psycho-analytical sense of *id* may have developed from the biological sense: in the latter, the Germanicism *id* abbreviates *idioplasma*. Popular usage, as often as not, omits *libido* and speaks of '*the ego* and *the id*', with the approximate meaning 'an individual's conscious personality, especially his conscious thinking, and (*the id*) his instincts, especially his instinctive impulses'. *Libido* comes, like *ego*, straight from Latin, where it denotes all desire but, particularly, sexual desire; and psycho-analytical *id* represents the Latin neuter pronoun *id*, it. This Latinism, probably 'coined' by Freud, serves to internationalize the German *es*, it, or rather *Es*, the 'it' of psychoanalysis.

It is, however, Jung who has devised the complementary terms *introvert* (abstract noun: *introversion*) and *extrovert* (abstract: *extroversion*), with variants *intravert* and *extravert*. Whereas the former person, literally 'turned inside', tends to live inwardly, to find his deepest satisfaction in things of the mind, for instance in fancy and imagination, and in things of the spirit, for instance by the exercise of his religion, the latter, literally 'turned outside', tends to live outwardly, to find his greatest pleasures in externalities, for instance games or sex or the exercise of his trade or craft or profession. The dreamer and the idealist are introverts, the 'hearty' is an extrovert. But most of us are sometimes introvert, sometimes extrovert: predominance, not exclusion, determines the type.

Without being in any sense or to any degree complementary, although parallel, to *introversion* and *extroversion*, are *inhibition* and *exhibitionism*, the former connoting an excessive self-restraint, the latter an excessive self-display: a holding-in and a holding-out. *Exhibitionism* belongs to general psychology, *inhibition* to psychiatry. The latter bears, indeed, two main senses, as in 'the inhibition of anxiety by the cultivation of devil-may-care', a deliberate restraint, and in 'to obtain artistic freedom by ridding oneself of inhibitions', the restraints imposed by early training and by habit. Compare *repression*, a 'pressing-back', the banishment, by one's ego, of an impulse or even a desire unacceptable by the ego and its consequent relegation to the subconscious mind, where it may become more dangerous than if it had been frankly admitted. Compare also *frustration*, rather the baffling than the outright, manifest defeat of one's designs or desires. 'When you say people are "frustrated", you mean they're emotionally unemployed,' as a very perceptive author, Michael Innes, has remarked in his 'thriller', *A Private View*, 1952. *Frustration* is an abstract noun, built upon *frustrat-*, the stem of *frustratus*, past participle of *frustrare*, to render useless, to deceive, to frustrate, a verb deriving from the adverb *frustra*, in vain. Roman etymologists related *frustra* to *fraus*, a wrong done to someone, hence specifically fraud or deceit: and they may well have been right; at least, no modern scholar has proved them to be wrong.

Different from, yet oddly akin to *frustration* is *fixation*, from Medieval Latin *fixatio*, oblique stem *fixation-*, a fixing, and the more recent verb, *fixate*, usually explained as derived from Latin *fixus*, past participle of *figere*, to drive in, e.g. a stake or a nail; occasionally explained as from Medieval *fixare* (itself from *fixus*), past participle *fixatus*; but probably explained best as a back-formation from *fixat(ion)*. In psychiatry, *fixation* means specifically a fixing, or stoppage, of immature desire upon a natural yet unsuitable person or, even, object, as in *mother fixation*; a person suffering thus from an arrested development of sexual or potentially sexual desire is said to be *fixated*, as in 'He is *fixated* upon his mother' or, more colloquially, 'He's mother-fixated'.

Obviously akin to *mother fixation* and *father fixation* are *the Oedipus complex* and *the Electra complex*. In the former, a boy is excessively attached to his mother and is also hostile, often very stupidly hostile, to his father; in the latter, a girl is excessively attached to her father and hostile to her mother. The former has been named after Oedipus (Greek *Oidipous*, of which the

4*

first element represents *oida*, I know), who, in Classical Mytho-
logy, unwittingly married his mother; the latter, after Electra
('the brilliant one': feminine of *ēlektōr*, an adjective), who was
most affectionately, but in no way reprehensibly, attached to
her father, Agamemnon.

To the layman the three best-known complexes are *persecution
complex*, *guilt complex* and *inferiority complex*. An *inferiority complex*
denotes, for psychiatrists, the entire range of one's ideas and
feelings about personal inferiority, not merely, as the ignorant
think, the abnormality arising from a *suppressed* sense of inferiority. But then *complex* (Latin *complexus*, a noun formed from
complectari, to embrace, hence to comprise: *com-*, with+*plectere*,
to weave or twist) does not, except to the ignorant, mean 'an
abnormal feeling or group of feelings': properly, it means 'the
entire field, or set, of ideas and feelings about a particular
person or object or emotion'—for instance, one's personal hero,
one's home, one's ambition; it refers to the entire system of
thoughts, emotions and, indeed, memories. This psycho-
analytic sense derives from the general psychological sense
exemplified in 'a new complex of habit' (Whitehead). Admittedly, psychiatrists have increasingly narrowed 'system' to
denote either a repressed or a subconscious system—sometimes
a system both repressed and subconscious—and to understand
this narrowed system as one which, unknown to the subject,
controls or goes far towards controlling his life.

From certain complexes to *manic depression* is but a short step,
for this type of depression has in it something resembling *mania*,
a word connected with *mind*. The adjective is *manic-depressive*.
Compare *psycholepsy*, an access of despair combined with *accidia*
or mental inertia; adjective, *psycholeptic*; subject of the access
or attack, *psycholept*: words formed on the analogy of *nympho-
lepsy*, an access of obsessive enthusiasm seizing a man infatuated
or possessed by a nymph—of *nympholeptic*—and of *nympholept*
(Greek *numpholeptos*), the victim of this 'fate worse than death'.
The elements *-lepsis*, *-leptic*, *-lept* derive from the Greek *lam-
banein*, to take, grasp, seize.

Very different from psycholepsy is *narcissism*, an unhealthy
obsession with oneself; he who suffers from it is a *narcissist*.

Clearly the origin lies in the myth of that handsome Greek youth *Narkissos*, Latin—hence European—*Narcissus*, who fell in love with his own reflection.

Here the *phobias* naturally fall into place. Roughly a *phobia* (adjective *phobic*, subject *phobe*) is an enduring and excessive, especially if also irrational, fear of some particular object or group of allied objects, as in *acrophobia*, a fear of heights, from Greek *akros*, at the farthest point, especially upward; *agoraphobia*, an excessive fear of crowded places, hence of crowds, from *agora*, a market-place; *pyrophobia*, a dread of *fire*, from *pur*, fire. The *phob-* element stands for the Greek *phobos*, fear.

In sharp contrast to *phobia* stands *trauma*, which in medicine denotes either a wound (Greek *trauma*, a wound) or the condition resulting from one, but in psychiatry denotes some perturbation, especially a severe mental shock, to which a neurosis is attributable; the adjective is *traumatic* (Greek *traumatikos*). The impact of the word upon modern fiction may be exemplified in, for instance, Michael Innes's *A Private View*, where, of the chief character, it is remarked that 'In the worst of these narrows he thought he was stuck for good; it was like some abominable Freudian dream of the trauma of birth'.

Perhaps more fundamental than even a very serious trauma is *paranoia*, a word adopted from Greek, where it means either madness, especially a grave mental derangement, or extreme folly of the sort one charitably explains by saying that the poor fellow must be mad; *paranoia* consists of *para*, beside, to the side of, (hence) apart from, beyond, and *noia*, an alteration of *nous*, mind. In psychiatry, however, *paranoia* means a mental disorder that, chronic in its incidence, is characterized always by delusions of grandeur, hence of persecution, and occasionally by hallucinations; the usual adjective is *paranoiac*—compare *maniac* from *mania*; and, like *maniac*, *paranoiac* serves also as a noun.

Less spectacular but more interesting than paranoia is *schizophrenia*, a psychosis marked by the subject's diminishing sense of reality, by his notable unawareness of the world around him, and consequently by the gradual decay of his character and, indeed, of his entire personality; it is allied to, but it does not necessarily become, insanity—a good psychiatrist can often arrest the progress of schizophrenia. The adjective is *schizophrenic*; the noun, either *schizophrenic* or *schizophrene*—colloquially 'a *schizo*'. Now, schizophrenia is what the popular press calls 'a split personality'; strictly, a personality is split when it exhibits very noticeable contradictions, and it only tends towards *schizophrenia*. The popular error arose very naturally, for *schizophrenia* literally means 'the condition of a divided mind': Greek *schizo-*, a combining-form from *schizein*, properly *skhizein*, to cleave in two, to split +*phrēn*, the mind +*-ia*, a medical suffix indicating a morbid or disordered condition. Once again, therefore, we are seeing an example of the fact that psychiatric nomenclature has occasionally been—well, shall we say 'infelicitous'? Usually it is good. More than once, it is both felicitous and picturesque.

Passing to matters less grave than paranoia and schizophrenia, we meet with *defence mechanism*, a mental device adopted by a subject (person)—usually unaware that he is doing so—for the achievement of some end, especially the gratification of a desire, and with *escapism* (adjective: *escapist*), by which a subject habitually and, as often as not, consciously occupies—above all, entertains—his mind in order to avoid thinking of unpleasant reality or merely to obviate the deadening effects of routine.

Escapism is manifestly akin to *wishful thinking*, which, normally adopted to ignore unpleasant facts or to render one's mental or emotional life more pleasant, consists either in believing to be true what one wishes to be true or in finding illusory confirmation of what one likes to believe or to think. It is dangerous only when it leads to ill-founded optimism. The late Olaf Stapledon, in that stimulating book, *Beyond the Isms*, 1942, could in one place write, 'Gradually scientific integrity, intellectual honesty, came to be felt as the supreme virtue, and wishful thinking became the deepest sin against the spirit', and in another, no less sincerely, 'My last word to the sceptic about the spirit is this. Let him earnestly examine his own heart. He has too easily cowed us by his air of superior intellectual integrity and by his imputation of confused and wishful thinking. It is time that we who recognize the spirit should have the courage of our convictions, and turn the tables on him.' Very few of those who cultivate the spirit need to consult a psychiatrist. Unfortunately, precious few cultivate the spirit; some don't even know that such a thing exists.

A very odd form of wishful thinking is the *death wish*, a morbid result of 'the Atomic Age' and of a consequent panic. Panic cannot supervene while the mind remains in control, nor while one realizes that the spirit is of greater importance than the body: a body exists, a spirit lives. Yet *death wish* and *wishful* (or as a wit has punned it, wistful) *thinking* possess a philological significance: amid the welter of grecized and latinized words, they stand out, lonely peaks, by their unaffected Englishry.

Wishful thinking, *escapism* and *defence mechanism* bring us to *sublimation*, the diversion, whether deliberate or subconscious, of a baffled aim or an unrealized desire into an occupation of a higher order; thus, the passion of love or the goad of lust can be diverted into creative work or, in the altruistic, into social works. *Sublimation* derives from Medieval Latin *sublimatio* (genitive *sublimationis*), from *sublimare*, to elevate, from *sublimis*, lofty, itself from *sub*, under, and *limen*, a lintel, with basic sense 'up to, hence on, the lintel'. Its adjective *sublimational—sublimatory* is non-psychological—is not to be confused with *subliminal*, literally below (*sub*) the threshold (*limen*). The Latin *limen* has the complementary senses 'lintel' and 'threshold'—a crosspiece at the head, a crosspiece at the foot, of a door. The *subliminal self* is that part of one's personality which lies below or, if you prefer, beyond his awareness: compare, therefore, *the subconscious*, both for the meaning and for the fact that laymen often misunderstand these fundamental words.

What then of those two other terms airily misused by laymen: *compensation* and *projection*? *Compensation*, literally a weighing together (L *compensatio*: *com-*, with, and a derivative from *pendere*, to weigh), denotes the act—or the result—of substituting something either agreeable or second-best for something disagreeable or unattainable; the technical adjective is *compensational*.

Projection is rather more tricky. Literally a throwing forward (*pro*+a combining form of Latin *iacere*, Medieval *jacere*, to throw), *projection* in its psychiatric application designates the extraordinarily convenient habit of attributing to other persons, or even to objects, one's own aims, desires, thoughts and especially one's own defects and faults; a habit sometimes identical with an over-zealous prosecution of the belief that 'attack is the best defence'. The adjective is *projective*.

Such mental habits as projection, compensation, sublimation, wishful thinking are 'human, all too human'. They have their comical side. They are much less dangerous than paranoia or schizophrenia.

But all the foregoing habits and tendencies, diseases and malaises, have one thing in common. They prevent or, at the least, threaten to prevent us from *integrating our personalities*. The *integrated personality*, result of the *integration of personality*, is the goal of all men of good will (*hommes de bonne volonté*) or men of *integrity*, whether psychiatrists or laymen. The *integrative* process means very much the same as the co-ordinative process; to *integrate* means little more than to co-ordinate. Nevertheless, *integration* connotes an element of internal—that is, of spiritual and intellectual—unification, whether in effort or in process or in result. To *integrate* is to render whole, all of a piece, unflawed, as, in fact, its etymology shows. 'To *integrate*' comes from *integratus* (stem *integrat-*), past participle of *integrare*, to make whole: *integrare* comes from *integer* (whence also, via Medieval *integralis*, the adjective *integral*), whole, entire, but literally untouched: *integer* combines *in-*, not, with an alteration of *tangere*, to touch, past participle *tactus*. Latin *integer*, English *integral* and *integrated*, should therefore be set beside Latin *intactus* and its English derivative *intact*. Comparatively, yet only comparatively *intact* and *integral* as we are at birth, we later find, especially when we reach middle age, that we have to *reintegrate* rather than *integrate* our personalities.

Psychiatry, it is clear, goes straight to psychological fundamentals. Naturally the language of psychiatry, represented inadequately yet not altogether unfairly in the preceding pages, leads us at times into deep waters. We need not drown in those waters.

AUSTRALIAN ENGLISH

AUSTRALIAN ENGLISH[1]

AUSTRALIAN English, like New Zealand and South African and even Canadian English, differs much less from British English than does American English. Yet American English resembles British English at far more points, and in more important respects, than those at (or in) which it differs. Australian English and British English are closer to each other than many Australians believe: and far closer than most Britons think.

The history of Australian English follows very much the same course as that followed by the English of the other dominions and also, indeed, by that of the United States of America. Mainly for political reasons, including the admission, to the United States, of millions of Continental Europeans, English has, in the U.S.A., diverged more sharply and more variously than in Australia and New Zealand, South Africa and Canada. In all those countries, English has had three great stages of development:

(1) at first, the settlers spoke the English they had spoken in Britain;

(2) only with the second generation did differences of accent and intonation, syntax and accidence appear to any marked degree and differences of vocabulary become numerous, and for many years the balance between British and Colonial English was held fairly evenly, with the latter slowly yet inevitably growing the stronger;

(3) once the Colonial influence became at last predominant, and the colonists perceived the predominance, that influence deepened and widened more rapidly than ever before. In the United States, the acceleration began with the signing, in 1776,

---

[1] This article appeared in a slightly different form, and without the chronological commentary, in *The Sunburnt Country*, 1953, and is printed here with the generous permission of Messrs William Collins. My article was written early in that year.

of the Declaration of Independence; in Australia, with the Federation in 1901. In both countries, however, any intelligent observer could, a generation earlier, have read the future, and only a fool would have failed to see the significance and importance of the manner of publication, as of the nature, of Henry Lawson's *Short Stories in Prose and Verse*, 1894.

The history of 'the Australian language' was at first synonymous with the history of settlement in Australia, from the arrival of the First Fleet at Botany Bay in 1788. 'Life ran thinly in the new world of the south in the years between 1788 and the end of the eighteenth century,' writes Sidney J. Baker in that valuable work, *The Australian Language*.[1] 'A few thousand people had been thrown together on the edge of a vast wilderness, before them the Pacific, behind them the grey, bleak unknown. They had scratched a toehold for themselves in a new land, and it was not much more than a toehold—a few huts, barracks for the convicts, the beginnings of cultivation, little else except the forbidding bush that pressed around them. . . . Yet out of that small fragment of a colony emerged the first glimpses of a new language.' Strictly, what emerged was a dialect; only in the second phase did that dialect become, in its more educated speakers, a variety of what the philologists, led by the late Professor H. C. K. Wyld, have agreed to call Modified Standard English: in this connexion, Standard Australian English.

But Australians have always made far too much of the convict element among the early settlers of Australia. After all, a large proportion of the early settlers of the United States of America consisted of malefactors transported to work on the plantations and elsewhere, yet we hear remarkably little about that proportion or even of that element. Americans have ignored the convict element, for excellent reasons: they don't give a damn; they realize that many of the convicts were com-

---

[1] 1st edition, 1945. Like myself, Sidney Baker is by birth a New Zealander; like myself, he owes much to the land of his adoption—and he has remained there. As Colonials, we understand and admire Australians; as New Zealanders we have perhaps gained something in detachment—a quality indispensable to historians.

paratively harmless; they know that life in a new country most
tremendously conditions the newcomers. In that admirable
book, *Australia* (1930), Professor W. K.—now Sir Keith—
Hancock, the best historian ever to have come out of what used
to be known as Australasia, has written some eloquent, some
extremely sensible, some fundamental pages on the subject. I
quote a short passage:

'Thanks to the stupid savagery of the penal code, some really
good raw material for nation building was transported to New
South Wales; there were among the convicts men of worth who
won for themselves an honourable place in colonial society.
Moreover, the most brutal of England's criminals were
generally sent to the gallows rather than to New South Wales.
So much may be conceded. But an examination of the record
of transportation at any period between 1790 and 1840 would
show that spirited poachers and political prisoners and even
picturesque intelligent villains were but a small leaven in the
lump, which was wretched and listless and forlorn. Were it
possible to compel the prison warders of this past age to produce
for our inspection a "typical" transported convict, they would
show us, not the countryman who snared rabbits, but the
Londoner who stole spoons.' It might also be remembered that,
except to Van Diemen's Land (Tasmania), the transportation
of convicts to Australia ceased in 1840; that at no time was the
proportion of females greater than one in five and that the
proportion of convicts, male or female, marrying and having
children was never more than one in twenty. For myself, I
should much prefer a great-great-grandfather transported for
stealing food in order to prevent his family from starving than a
grandfather enriched by cornering a market or by swindling
thousands of decent people by shady financial operations.

The subject of convictism has, however, been emphasized
less for its social than for its linguistic importance. Both Sir
Keith Hancock and Mr Sidney Baker have drawn attention to
the rather large number of underworld terms that were adopted
by or that seeped into the everyday speech of the general
population of Australia during the first forty years; but the
number is proportionately not much larger than in England

itself. Language has always in part recruited itself from below as well as from above and, most numerously, from all sides.

No; the most important linguistic feature of the underworld influence in early Australia is not the number of words and phrases it introduced into the staple of Australian speech—hence, though necessarily less, of Australian writing—but the more subtle and more pervasive results of the numerical pre-dominance of convicts, emancipated convicts, and the cul-turally little superior soldiery and minor officials (e.g., warders) over the free, non-military, non-official population until *ca.* 1830. Those results[1] were as follows.

Australian speech and writing have, from the outset, tended to be unconventional. By 'unconventional' I am not referring to morals; of all the Colonies that became Dominions it is probably true that, except perhaps during the first generation, the inhabitants are more 'proper', both in speech and in writing, than Englishmen and Englishwomen. The unconventionality is linguistic. It issues in a freer interpretation and a simpler practice of accidence and syntax, in a readier acceptance of new terms, in a healthy, only very rarely lawless, contempt for the social strata of language, and in a greater facility of metaphor-coining and of word-coining.

Australian English has always been or, at the least, either consciously striven or subconsciously worked to become natural, unaffected, sincere, direct and therefore, all in all, simple. We clearly see this tendency and this aim already in Marcus Clarke and Henry Kendall and T. A. Browne; we even detect its beginnings in such English visitors or residents as Wakefield and Cunningham and Henry Kingsley; in Henry Lawson and 'Banjo' Patterson, this simplicity, this directness and this naturalness have fully bloomed. Nor has the bloom they imparted during the last six years of the nineteenth de-parted in the twentieth century, although it has, since *ca.* 1942, become considerably more sophisticated. Convicts and warders

[1] It is impossible to seize and pin down and adequately describe such intangibles and imponderables. The results are more numerous, less exact, than my diagnosis might lead the layman to suppose; but they are certainly not less—if anything they are more—powerful than I state or even imply.

and soldiers and those genuine as well as those riff-raff adventurers who, once free immigration became possible, began to arrive, naturally preferred the direct and the unadorned; often they insisted upon it.

To all such men, the open air connoted freedom: not only the major freedom of free men, a freedom that to most of the early inhabitants formed a mere aspiration, but also the minor and temporary freedom gained by being outside the confines of the barrack-prisons. Life in the open air became gradually a national ideal and a literary fundamental.

Hatred of restraint led, as we have seen, to unconventionality: freedom, or the desire of freedom, from restraint influenced not merely vocabulary and style and speech but also the choice of subjects and the selection of the characters in poetry, in fiction, in newspaper articles. The convict in *For the Term of His Natural Life* differs from the convict—whether 'hero' or minor character—in any earlier novel written in English. In a new land, proportions change: men's speech changes: and the writings narrating or describing the land and the men (and women) inevitably and very rapidly change along with the strange scene, the climate, the entire social background.

Thus we come to what most writers on Australia and, previously, all writers upon 'the Australian language' have treated as the earliest and most important factor: the alien soil; the different climate; the strange flora and fauna; even the different geographical and topographical features; the aboriginals; the unaccustomed needs and consequently the new habits and occupations; moreover, arising from these physical media, and constantly shaped and shaded by them, are the psychological, intellectual and spiritual concomitants: an individuality more rugged than rough, an individuality strong and clear-cut; an independence at once sturdy and manly, self-reliant and self-promoting, courageous and persevering; a quiet, wryly humorous acceptance of the buffetings of fate in the dread form of drought and bush-fires, of sudden floods and other unpredictable forces; conversely, a warm appreciation of Nature's bounty when bounty it is; a scathing contempt of sham and hypocrisy, of pretence and pretentiousness; an intense dislike of pomposity and protocol; a pride of country more patent yet no less genuine than that of an Englishman or a Scot, a Welshman or an Irishman—a pride all the more natural, all the stronger, for being directed at a country that became its inhabitants' home-land 'the hard way'; a slightly sardonic humour, natural enough in those who have experienced the sardonicisms of a land often greyly bleak or cruelly bright; a tremendous respect for the first-rate, sympathy and friendliness towards the second-rate, and impatience with the third-rate; a very marked resourcefulness and adaptability, not only existing among those who, on the land, would probably fail to survive without them but also extending, perhaps as an inherited racial trait, to city-dwellers. A constant listening to the wind rustling the eucalypts ('gum trees') and the acacias ('wattles') and soughing about the surrealist cactus ('prickly pear') and in the mulga grass has refined the national ear; generations of exposure to the Australian climate have produced great singers and a timbre and an accent that somewhat resemble those of South Africa, a country similarly placed geographically.

In what have the physical background, geography and topography of Australian civilization, the fauna and flora, and all that goes with them—in what and to what extent have they influenced the language? The most obvious influence has been on the vocabulary, every new quadruped, bird, fish, reptile—flower, tree, shrub, grass—and such physiographical features as *billalong* and 'the *mallee*' and 'the *big scrub*'—the aboriginal (familiarly *abo*) and words connected with his way of life, e.g. *humpy, gunyah, mia-mia, wurley* (these four words denote a native hut), *waddy* (cudgel:? pidgin for 'wood'), *nulla-nulla, boomerang, woomera, cooee, corroboree, gin* and *lubra*.

One or other of the aboriginal dialects has accounted for such other Australianisms as

Animal life: *boomah, kangaroo, wallaby* and *wallaroo, koala* and *bandicoot* and *wombat, warrigal* and *dingo*, the fabulous *bunyip*; *kookaburra, galah, budgerigar*; *dugong, yabby, burramundi*.

Plant life: *mulga* and *geebung*, *boobyalla* and *boree*, *kurrajong* and *gidyah*, *coolibah* and *brigalow* and *burrawang*—and several dozen others.

Customs, Habits, Rites: *bogie* (to bathe), *bora*, *coolaman*.

Miscellaneous: *billy* (as in *boil the billy*), *dilly*, *jackaroo*, *jumbuck*, *myall*, *pindan*, *wamba*.

Two or three of those words may have perhaps a European, not an Australian origin; most of those words are very seldom heard outside Australia; nevertheless, all those words form an integral part of the Australian vocabulary. The most generally used words refer mainly to the land or to those who, including the aboriginals, are vitally concerned with it.

In the early history of Australia and its language there are several other aspects worth considering; they arise from the life of the pioneers and the gold-diggers, the adventurous farmers and the bushrangers. Among the more notable terms we find *bushranger* itself, with its *bail up* or *stick up*; *cattle duffing* and *cattle duffer*, *horse duffing*, *duffing yard*, where *duff*, to steal, has been taken over from the speech of the underworld; *gully-raking* and *scrub-running*, the search, in *gulleys* (gorges and wild valleys) and *scrub* (land covered with thick bushes or even with gum trees), for stock, especially cattle, to steal; *squatter*; *stockrider*, *stockwhip*, *stockyard*; *runs* or *stations*, for (very) large sheep or cattle farms or ranches, the original forms being *stock-run*, now archaic, or *sheep-run*, still heard occasionally, and *stock(-)station*, now obsolete; *cockatoo* (*farmer*), superseded, ca. 1890, by *cocky;* *selection*, a small farm in a district thrown open by the government; the *backblocks*, district(s) remote from the amenities of urban civilization; *the never-never land* or *country*, usually *the never-never*, back of beyond; *creek*, a brook or a stream larger than a brook, yet smaller than a river—a usage very common also in Canada and the United States and fairly common in New Zealand; *the bush*, scrub-grown country, hence loosely, among city-dwellers only, any farming district; *to be bushed* or lost; *bushwhacker*, colloquial for a *bushman*, one who lives in the *bush*; *bush telegraph*, the means whereby bushrangers kept themselves well informed, hence the spreading of news and rumours, but also a synonym of 'the grapevine'; *paddock*, a field of any size up to 50,000 acres or so; *jackaroo*, a tenderfoot station-hand, hence any station-hand, may have been an aboriginal word but more probably blends the *Jacky* of *Jacky* (or *Johnny*) *Raw*, a newcomer, with (kang)*aroo*; *roustabout*, a handyman on a station, especially in the *woolshed* (shearing-shed) for the *ringers* (fastest shearers) and would-be *ringers*; *bullocky*, a bullock driver; *clearskins* or *cleanskins*, unbranded cattle; '*poddy*(-*calf*), a calf just taken from its mother; *ropeable*, applied to cattle that are controllable only with a rope, hence slangily to persons extremely angry; (of a horse) to *buck*, hence *buck-jumping*; *brumby*, a horse born or become wild, and living untamed, either from a horsebreeder named *Brumby* or from a Queensland aboriginal *boorambie* or *baroombie* (the one word being a metathesis of the other); *boundary-riders* and *overlanders*, the latter conducting stock for great distances, shorter distances being covered by drovers—a distinction that cannot be pressed very closely; the *swagman*, colloquially *swaggie*, is also called a *sundowner*, because this species of tramp tries, usually with success, to reach a station at or about sunset, although the latter term, as in Jon Cleary's *The Sundowners*, has latterly been applied also to such a shearer or station-hand or general handyman as travels about the country and sleeps usually in a tent.

Gold-digging has given us *digger*, short for *gold-digger*. Originally an occupational term of address—compare the use of *Soldier* and *Sailor*—it had, well before 1900, become a general form of address among men; hence, in the war of 1914-18, the *Diggers* were the Australian soldiers. Also from the (gold-) *diggings* have come *fossick*, to search for something, to look *about* for it; hence *fossicker*, a 'scavenger' for gold; *hatter*, a lone-man miner, hence a lonely dweller in *the outback*, is explained by Edward A. Morris as 'one who has everything under his own hat' but is more naturally explained as deriving from 'mad as a hatter'; *shicer* and *duffer*, both meaning an unproductive mine, come ultimately from the underworld; to *salt* a useless claim or mine with gold dust or small nuggets.

Some of the gold-diggers were tramps, 'dead-beats', wanderers, itinerants working only sporadically and under the direst obligation, and several terms connected with them are worth recording—in addition to the already mentioned *sundowner* and *swaggie*: *battler*, because he battles his way through life, as in Kylie Tennant's notable sociological novel, *The Battlers*; *toe-ragger*, a dead-beat wanderer, from the rags worn instead of socks; the obsolete *Murrumbidgee whaler*, a man unusually lazy, even for a tramp, from basking on the shores of that river and boasting about the enormous fish he didn't catch; *on the wallaby* (*track* understood), on tramp; *waltzing Matilda* (noun), carrying a swag—a 'jazzed up' distortion of *walking Matilda*, where *Matilda* affectionately refers to the swag, much as *Liz* or *Lizzie* does to a type of motorcar; *bluey*, a swag, from the blue, or the grey striped with blue, blanket carried by the tramp; *scale a rattler*, to jump a train.

It would probably be impossible, it would certainly be tedious, to furnish an adequate selection of the terms added to the language by every succeeding cultural wave. It is, however, fitting to mention the main influences operating after the gold-rush days. They are:

The further opening-up of the country, not only by exploration but also by gradual settlement.

The constant antiphony—the physical contrast and the spiritual conflict—between town and country, for in no other land does so high a proportion of the population live in the large cities, an alarming number in the State capitals alone: a vast subject this, worthy of a doctorate either in economics or in linguistics, for its intellectual and cultural implications are numerous and extremely complex, not to say complicated.

The Boer War (1899–1902), World War One (1914–18) and World War Two (1939–45) have considerably affected Australians, whether they served abroad or served at home, often by rendering them sharply conscious of the merits and advantages of their own country; which brings us to——

Australian nationalism, first inculcated intensively by W. J. Archibald, founder of *The Bulletin*; an unusual nationalism, for it has an unmistakably dualistic nature, combining a fierce loyalty to Australia with, especially in times of emergency, an indefeasible loyalty to the Crown. Very few Australians understand this dualism: it would ill become an outsider to attempt an analysis.

The cinema, at the end of the nineteenth century with the 'talkies' coming some thirty years later, and then radio, from the early 1920's, have considerably influenced Australian speech and vocabulary, as they have influenced those of almost every other civilized country.

Americanization, detectable in the large cities ever since *ca.* 1910, has spread with the increase of the cinema habit and notably since 1942, the year in which the American invasion began. This rapidly increasing Americanization has something, admittedly difficult to analyse and impossible to assess, to do with recent trends in Australian nationalism. The Americanization has come not only from cinema and radio, books and magazines, but also from the adroit employment of American capital and from the residence and visits of American businessmen.

Periodicals have, from early days and as an inevitable or, at the least, entirely natural result of the preponderance of gazettes and other periodicals over books for at least two generations, exercised in Australia an influence far greater than that exercised by books. Without labouring the point, one may remark that this newspaper influence has powerfully and intimately affected the character of Australian speech as well as of Australian writing, especially towards a reduction of the literary and artistic, the aesthetic and intellectual, elements in speech and writing. That reduction is sometimes, although by no means always, a very good thing.

The preceding paragraph should lead us into an attempt to describe the general characteristics of Australian English, but that must come later, for here, not altogether ineptly, one must interpose a paragraph or so on Australian pronunciation.

Australian pronunciation depends upon, indeed it has been

conditioned by, exactly the same two great factors as have determined the development and then largely established the nature of every kind of what was originally some Colonial English or other—American, Canadian, South African, Australian, New Zealand, to take them in the chronological order of the foundation of the respective colonies: the racial and the climatic.[1] In short, the processes that have gone to form Australian pronunciation were, like the results, inevitable.

First, the racial factor. The earliest inhabitants of Botany Bay were predominantly English, with a few from Wales, Scotland and Ireland; of the Englishmen, a high proportion came from London. Until late in the nineteenth century, few foreigners settled in Australia. When foreigners did begin to arrive in any numbers, Germans, French, Italians and, among Asiatics, Chinese led the way. But Australia never became a racial melting-pot as the United States, and, rather less, Canada have done. The preponderating racial or, if you prefer it, linguistic influence has been British, especially English, with that of London very noticeable.

But more important is the climatic or, if you prefer it, the environmental influence. Climate and physical surroundings have gradually shaped Australian pronunciation into something decidedly *sui generis*, quite distinct even from South African. Nothing much has been done, and it has been done rather late in the day, to modify it. But a people has full rights to its own speech: to leave it as it is, and glory in it; or to modify it. What is to be deprecated is that Australians should be so very accent-conscious. They can either preserve their ancient speech and, like the Americans, think, perhaps even say, 'This is ours, and we like it. If you don't like it, you know what to do about it,'— or they can set about modifying it. The decision rests entirely with *them*.

After saying something, for I obviously had to say something, on that extremely thorny subject (Englishmen, by the way, think that Australians attribute to pronunciation an importance

[1] Those who prefer a more formal treatment will go to either or preferably both of Professor A. G. Mitchell's or Mr Sidney Baker's books on Australian pronunciation.

considerably greater than it has), I turn with relief to a rather
less thorny, though still slightly prickly, subject: the general
characteristics of Australian English. But before doing so I
should like to add that the British attitude perhaps has something in its favour. Britons are neither proud nor ashamed of
their pronunciation (accent, intonation, pitch): they take it
for granted. Nor are they much concerned with exterior
criticism, whether favourable or neutral or adverse, of their
pronunciation; they do, however, take pains with it.

The principal characteristics of 'the Australian language' are,
it seems to me, the following:

'A marked feature of "low-browism" in our speech—a
deliberate speaking-down, an avoidance of polish and
finesse in speech, the adoption of a hard-boiled, to-hell-
with-the-King's-English view' (Sidney J. Baker). But that
aspect of 'speaking-down' which consists in understate-
ment is generically British, not particularly Australian.
Yet what's wrong with subtlety and suppleness and
educated, cultured speech—and especially with cultured,
educated, supple, subtle writing, provided that these qualities do not (there's no compulsion why they should) impair,
much less destroy, clarity and vigour? To relinquish all
such shades of meaning as possess intellectual, moral,
spiritual significance and importance would be defeatist
and degrading. Yet Australians are no more defeatist, no
more degraded than any other people: so why pretend to
worship things that, if pursued for any length of time,
would render them, not a people respected, as indeed they
are, but something rather different? Directness is a virtue;
it is, however, a virtue less valuable than clarity and
adequacy.
A marked dependence upon and use of slang in speech and
even in writing. The use is excessive, the dependence unfortunate. But—this is a truly tremendous 'but'—the best
Australian writers, be they historians or essayists, poets or
novelists or short-story writers, publicists or journalists,
use no more slang than the best English, Scottish, Welsh,

Irish writers and slightly less than the best American.

The tendency of Australian humour to be sardonic or ironic. 'The native-born joke . . . comes pat, faintly mocking, hiding a sting in its tail,' as the late Dr Thomas Wood remarked in *Cobbers* (1934).

The Cockney and American influences and elements, the former rapidly decreasing, the latter rapidly increasing, have, like the aboriginal element rather than influence, been sufficiently dealt with in earlier pages.

Australian syntax tends to discard all the subtleties of English syntax and several subtleties of English accidence. Yet the greatest Australian writers do not lack subtlety, discrimination, finesse, variety.

A far greater ability of Australian writers in prose than in verse, and a very clearly marked tendency in the Australian public to refrain from reading verse. The latter characteristic is merely a characteristic of the human race; in all the British Dominions, as also in the United States of America, this tendency is even more potent than it is in Britain.

The disappearance of such English words as *field* and *lea* and *meadow*, *brook* and *rivulet*, *glen* and *coomb*, *vale* and *dale*, *wood* (forest) and *thicket*, *mere* and *pond*, *copse* and *spinney*, *fen* and *marsh*, *knoll* and *mound*, and also of such words as *village* and *hamlet*, *inn* and *hostelry*.

The disappearance of such honorifics as *sir* and *madam*, and of *Esq(uire)* after a name.

The tendency of the spoken vocabulary to be much, that of the written vocabulary to be very slightly, smaller than that of an Englishman or a Scot or an Irishman of approximately the same education or culture or social standing.

But, on the other hand, a greater facility and a much slighter self-consciousness about the coining and using of new metaphors or of 'outlandish' speech: in short, a readier welcome to linguistic originality, although not (I believe) to literary, artistic, musical originality.

A tendency to dismiss expatriates as 'a dead loss'. Yet such writers as, to mention only a few, Martin Boyd, Godfrey Blunden, James Aldridge, Jack Lindsay and Chester

Wilmot bring perhaps more credit to Australia by living abroad than they would by living at home. No country much cares to see its native talent going elsewhere: and clearly there must be a limit to such migration. But Australia does not lose its writers, painters, musicians when they go abroad: she merely lends them. She might, however, ask herself why so many of those who temporarily leave her shores, never or only briefly return to them. A country gets the poets and painters, the musicians and novelists, the sculptors and historians she deserves. Like love, creative merit has to be encouraged, nurtured, sustained. In common with all the other Dominions, Australia perhaps does less than she might for these creators, who, even in a democracy, do, after all, merit a little material encouragement and moral sustenance.

CHRONOLOGICAL COMMENTARY

The following works form the main landmarks in the history, description and lexicography of Australian English:

1880　*The* (Sydney) *Bulletin*, founded by J. F. Archibald. The case-book of Australian English.

1898　E. A. Morris, *Austral English*, with an introduction. A good, though rather too English, piece of work. An up-to-date dictionary of Australian English—standard, colloquial, slang—is being prepared, with a long critical introduction, by Professor A. G. Mitchell of the University of Sydney.

1898　*Webster's International Dictionary*, with a special supplement, by Joshua Lake, of Australian terms.

1900–10　S. E. O'Brien and A. G. Stephens, 'Material for a Dictionary of Australian Slang'—a typescript in the Mitchell Library, Sydney.

1926　'Jice Doone' (Vance Marshall), *Timely Tips to New Australians*. Slang and colloquial terms only; a good introduction.

1932   Nettie Palmer, (a chapter in) *Talking It Over*.
1933   Eric Partridge, *Slang Today and Yesterday* (3rd edition, revised, 1951).
1933   (September)–(January) 1934   L. G. D. Acland, *Sheep-Station Glossary*, published in *The Press* (an important New Zealand newspaper).
1937   Eric Partridge, *A Dictionary of Slang and Unconventional English*, 3rd edition, revised and much enlarged, 1949; 5th edition, revised and still further enlarged, 1961.
1943   Sidney J. Baker, *A Popular Dictionary of Australian Slang*, an enlarged edition.
1945   Sidney J. Baker, *The Australian Language* (since revised).
1946   A. G. Mitchell, *The Pronunciation of English in Australia*.
1947   Sidney J. Baker, *Australian Pronunciation*.
1950   Eric Partridge, *A Dictionary of the Underworld*, enlarged edition, 1960.
1951   Eric Partridge and John W. Clark, *British and American English since 1900*, relevant chapter by Andrew Thompson.
1953   Sidney J. Baker, *Australia Speaks*.
1960   Sidney J. Baker, *The Drum*.

And then there are the periodicals and writers that, in fact as opposed to theory, have the most influenced or the best exemplified the growth, nature and potentialities of written and, though inevitably less, of spoken Australian English, whether Standard or non-Standard:

1819   Barron Field, *First Fruits of Australian Poetry*. Intrinsically negligible, extrinsically worth recording.
1827   Peter Cunningham, *Two Years in New South Wales*. This Scottish naval surgeon, 'a man of remarkable powers of observation' (D.N.B.), was not the first nor will he be the last to write such a work: he was merely one of the two or three best.
1831–   *The Sydney Morning Herald*, which set and has maintained a standard.
1833–   *The West Australian*.
1840–   *The* (Melbourne) *Herald*.
1842–   *The* (Launceston) *Examiner*.

1846–   *The* (Melbourne) *Argus*.

1854–   *The* (Melbourne) *Age*.

1854–   *The* (Hobart) *Mercury*.

1858–   *The* (Adelaide) *Advertiser*.

1859   Henry Kingsley, *The Recollections of Geoffrey Hamlyn*. In the British-Australian convention.

1862–80   Henry Kendall, *Poems and Songs*, 1862; *Leaves from Australian Forests*, 1869; *Songs from the Mountains*, 1880.

1865–   *The Australian Journal*.

1867–70   Adam Lindsay Gordon, *Sea Spray and Smoke Drift*, 1867, and *Bush Ballads and Galloping Rhymes*, 1870.

1867–1926   *The* (Sydney) *Evening News*.

1869–97   Marcus Clarke, from *Long Odds*, 1869, through (later, *The Term of*) *His Natural Life*, 1874, to *Stories of Australia in the Early Days*, 1897.

1872–   *The* (Brisbane) *Telegraph*.

1878–1905   'Rolf Boldrewood' (T. A. Browne), from *Ups and Downs*, 1878, through *Robbery under Arms* (1881 in *The* Sydney *Mail*, 1888 in book-form), *A Sydney-Side Saxon*, 1891, and *In Bad Company*, 1901, to *The Last Chance*, 1905. Like Gordon, English-born, but far more 'Australianized' than Kingsley and Gordon.

1880–   *The* (Sydney) *Bulletin*, with its world-famous 'Red Page'; to it the majority of the best Australian journalists and authors have, since its inception, contributed.

1884–   *The* (Sydney) *Daily Telegraph*, since 1936 simply *Daily Telegraph*.

1890–1905   E. W. Hornung's Australian period: *A Bride from the Bush*, 1890; *The Boss of Taroomba*, 1894; *Dead Men Tell No Tales*, 1899; *Stingaree*, 1905.

ca. 1893–1914   A. G. Stephens, *A Queenslander's Travel Notes*, 1894, but then mostly in *The Bulletin*. A fine journalist.

1894–1922: Henry Lawson, best period 1894–1905, from *Short Stories in Prose and Verse*, 1894, through *When the World was Wide*, and *While the Billy Boils*, both in 1896, *On the Track and over the Sliprails*, 1900, *Joe Wilson and His Mates*, 1901, to *When I was King*, 1905. The first truly, at all points, Australian writer.

1896-1904 effective period of A. B. ('Banjo') Paterson: *The Man from Snowy River*, 1896; *Rio Grande's Last Race*, 1904. A thoroughly Australian version of Adam Lindsay Gordon.

1896-1930 John Le Gay Brereton, the Younger (scholar, poet, essayist): *The Song of Brotherhood*, 1896; *Elizabethan Drama*, 1909; *Swags Up!*, 1928; *Knocking Around*, 1930. His father, whose poetic work covered the period 1857–1887 and whose best work was *The Triumph of Love*, 1887, was hardly Australian at all.

1896-1907 best Australian period of Louis Becke: from *A First Fleet Family* to *The Settlers of Karossa Creek*.

1899 'Steele Rudd' (A. H. Davis), *On Our Selection*. It put the 'cocky' on the map.

1901-39 Miles Franklin, e.g. *My Brilliant Career*, 1901; *Old Blastus of Bandicoot*, 1931; *All that Swagger*, 1936; with Dymphna Cusack, *Pioneers on Parade*, 1939.

1903 'Tom Collins' (Joseph Furphy), *Such Is Life*. A notably Australian book.

1903-41 Bernard O'Dowd, from *Dawnward*, 1903, through *The Silent Land*, 1905, *The Bush*, 1912, and *Alma Venus*, 1921, to the collected edition of his poems, 1941.

1905-29 (effective novel-writing period of) 'Henry Handel Richardson' (Mrs J. G. Robertson)—*Maurice Guest*, 1905; *The Getting of Wisdom*, 1910; *Australian Felix*, 1917, *The Way Home*, 1925, and *Ultima Thule*, 1929, the trilogy *The Fortunes of Richard Mahony* appearing in 1930.

1906 Edward Dyson, *Fact'ry 'Ands*. Established the larrikin.

1908 Jeannie (Mrs Aeneas) Gunn, *We of The Never Never*. Explained the Outback to those who knew it not.

1908-39 'William Blocksidge' (William Baylebridge), *Songs o' the South*, 1908, *Australia to England*, 1909, *Love Redeemed*, 1934, and *Sextains*, 1939—poems; *An Anzac Muster*, 1921—tales.

1911 Louis Stone, *Jonah*.

1913-18 Christopher Brennan, *Poems*, 1913; *A Chant of Doom*, 1918.

1915-50 Katharine Susannah Prichard, as in *The Pioneers*,

5

1915; *Working Bullocks*, 1926; *Haxby's Circus*, 1930; *The Roaring Nineties*, 1946; *Winged Seeds*, 1950.

1916   (Sir) Ernest Scott, *A Short History of Australia.*

1916–17 C. J. Dennis's *Sentimental Bloke* and *Ginger Mick.*

1920   Louis Esson, *Dead Timber, and Other Plays.*

1921–37 C. E. W. Bean's share in the history of the A.I.F. in 1914–18.

1923   'Rann Daly', *The Enchanted Island*, 1923, and *The Outpost*, 1924; then as himself, Vance Palmer, e.g. *Separate Lives*, 1931, and *Golconda*, 1948.

1928   Martin Boyd, *The Montforts* (pseudonymous); *Night of the Party*, 1938; *Lucinda Brayford*, 1946; *The Cardboard Crown*, 1952; *A Difficult Young Man*, 1955; *Outbreak of Love*, 1957. One of the six best of all Australian novelists.

1929   'M. Barnard Eldershaw' (Flora Eldershaw and Majorie Barnard), *A House Is Built.*

1929–   Norman Lindsay as novelist, as in *The Cautious Amorist*, 1932. (His talented sons Jack and Philip have written almost entirely upon non-Australian themes.)

1930   W. K. (now Sir Keith) Hancock, *Australia.*

1931–   Frank Dalby Davison, e.g. *Man-Shy* ('a story of men and cattle'), 1931; *Dusty* ('the story of a sheep dog'), 1946.

1934   Archer Russell, *A Tramp-Royal in Wild Australia.*

1934   Thomas Wood, *Cobbers*. Like the preceding, a distinguished piece of work.

1935–51 Brian Penton, first (1935–36) as novelist, then as journalist (*Think—or be Damned*, 1941).

1935–   Godfrey Blunden, especially in *No More Reality*, 1935.

1936–   (Ellen) Dymphna Cusack, *Jungfrau* (a novel), 1936; plays; with Florence James, *Come in Spinner*, 1951; *Southern Steel*, 1953.

1939–   Kylie Tennant, e.g. *Foveaux*, 1939, *The Battlers*, 1941, *Lost Haven*, 1947, and *The Joyful Condemned*, 1953; *The Honey Flow*, 1956.

1942–   James Aldridge, e.g. *Signed with Their Honour*, 1942; *Of Many Men*, 1946; *The Diplomat*, 1949; *The Hunter*, 1950; *Heroes of the Empty View*, 1954. (Non-Australian matter but virile manner.)

1942– Gavin Casey, e.g. *It's Harder for Girls*, 1942, and *City of Men*, 1950.

1944 Lawson Glassop, *We Were the Rats*. Also *Lucky Palmer*, 1948.

1946– Jon Cleary, *These Small Glories*, 1946; *You Can't See Round Corners*, 1949; *The Sundowners*, 1952; *The Climate of Courage*, 1954; *Back of Sunset*, 1959.

1948– Ruth Park, beginning with *The Harp in the South*.

1953 Erle Wilson, *Coorinna* (a novel); *Minado*, 1955; *Adams of the Bounty*, 1958.

1955 D'Arcy Niland, *The Shiralee*; *The Big Smoke*, 1959.

ETYMOLOGICAL

IMAGINATION AND GOOD SENSE
IN ETYMOLOGY

ETYMOLOGY, like philology in general, stands at a cross-roads:
either it can continue to make inductions from defective
premisses and then make deductions from those perhaps faulty
inductions, or it can apply, now the brake of that extremely
rare quality, good sense, now the spur of an imagination not yet
desiccated by a too strict adhesion to those so-called 'laws'
which are so obviously nothing more grandiose, nothing more
fundamental, nothing more compulsive than 'statements of
average'. Certain scholars have begun to recognize the need to
let in a little fresh air.

I have selected one theory and five etymologies as illustrations, not dogmatic but tentative and inceptive, of what I
mean. The theory bears upon a thesis put forward in America
just before the war: that the Indo-European languages
originated in Georgia—the ancient Iveria. They may have done
so. But I suspect that, wherever (perhaps Georgia) they first
constituted a core or a nexus, they formed only one of three
linguistic families having a common stock—a language common to the entire Mediterranean basin—which radiated north
to Greece and the Black Sea hinterlands, thence west and east,
to become the Indo-European group; east to the Levant, and
on to Arabia, to form the Semitic group; and south to North
Africa, to form the Hamitic group. Otherwise it is difficult to
account for the stems, and roots or radicals, and etymons that are
common to Indo-European, Semitic, Hamitic; words perhaps
too numerous to be explained away as borrowings. That is not a
theory to be dismissed summarily with raised eyebrow and
shrugged shoulder.

Then there are two echoic or, at the least, 'representative'
words that deserve a little more attention than they have
received: *atman*, the breath, hence the principle of life, hence
the individual soul, hence the universal soul, hence, as *Atman*,

Brahma, the Supreme Being of Hinduism; and *gas*. Ignored by
The Oxford English Dictionary and by *Weekley*, *atman* is stated by
The American College Dictionary to be a Sanskrit word and more
fully by *Webster's New International Dictionary* to derive from
Sanskrit *ātman*, breath, and to be akin to German *Atem*, breath.
But why not go further and link *ātman* (*ātma-n*) to the Greek
word for vapour, a word arising, of course, much later than the
Sanskrit word: to *atmos* (*atmo-s*)? We have only to look at, and
then say aloud, the Sanskrit stem *ātma-* in order to realize that
here is an echoic word, perhaps the most significantly echoic
word ever made by man: *āt* (pronounced approximately *aht*)—
a strong, slow in-breathing; *ma*, a strong, quick out-breathing:
inhalation and exhalation: the very breath of life. For the
semantics (language in its aspect of sense-development) we have
only to compare the less, though indubitably, echoic Latin
spiritus, a breathing, whence *Spiritus Sanctus*, the Holy Spirit.

Gas has received less cavalier treatment. 'Invented' by a
Dutch chemist, J. B. van Helmont (1677–1744), who admitted
its source in the Greek *kháos*, chaos, it seems to have had, ultimately, a somewhat similar origin, for one of its earliest senses is
'atmosphere'; the sense 'gaping abyss or opening' came later.
Admittedly, however, such scholars as Boisacq relate *kháos* to a
presumed Indo-European stem *gheu* or *ghou* or *ghu*, basic sense
'to gape', rather than postulate *kháos* to be a 'broadening' of a
presumed *khas*. If, by one chance in a myriad, I should happen
to be right, Greek *kháos* would be akin to *ghost*, Old English
gāst, breath, spirit, soul, and Old Saxon *gēst*, spirit, soul; that
the *-t* is not fundamental, I deduce from Gothic 'us*gais*jan'
and Old Norse '*geiske*'.

To pass to a word of a different order, why is it so persistently
stated that the transition of English *noise*, from Old French
noise, noise, din, from Latin *nausea* (adopted by English), from
Greek *nausía*, sea-sickness, itself from *naus*, a ship, presents a
grave semantic difficulty? A boat-load of passengers, caught
in a storm battering one of those small vessels of Ancient Greece,
must have made their *nausía* elementarily manifest by their
groans of physical distress and their outcries of fear: their
expression of *nausía* would have been extremely noisy; hence

the derivative sense, 'noise indicative of sea-sickness'; hence, 'loud noise, a din'; hence, any *noise*.

With *Cockney*, from *ca.* 1600, a Londoner, from *cockney*, a milksop (as in Chaucer), hence a townsman, we have a problem of another kind. The O.E.D. derives the 'milksop' sense from Middle English *cokeney* or *cokenay*, which appears to compound *coken*, of cocks, and *ey*, *ay*, an egg, and therefore to mean literally 'a cocks' (hence, 'a cock's') egg'; *cock's egg* is or was a name often given to a small, misshapen egg. If one can accept the very considerable semantic gap between the idea of such an egg and that of a milksop, the rest of the development is easy and natural. But many etymologists refuse to accept it, and the best alternative is that which was proposed by Ernest Weekley more than thirty years ago and which has been adopted by *Webster's*. Professor Weekley derives ME *cokeney*, *cokenay*, from a dialect form (*k* for *qu*) of Old French *acoquinei* (Modern Fr *acoquiné*), 'made into a *coquin* or rogue'; *acokinei* being apprehended as 'a *cokinei*', as he thinks, or merely shortened by aphesis to *cokinei*, *cokenei*, as I prefer. *Coquin* itself is of obscure origin; *Webster* suggests that it may come from Middle Low German *kak*, a pillory; perhaps rather it comes from an Indo-European *kak-* (with variant *kok-*), whence the Greek *kakos*, bad, evil, for the countryman thinks of the townsman no less often as a rogue— compare the American 'city slicker'—than as a milksop.

Another puzzling word is *phoney*, spurious, counterfeit. Britons became familiar with it when, late in 1939, they saw *the phoney war* applied by American journalists to the war in Europe. The etymologies proposed have been these: *Webster's*, tentatively, *funny*, as in '*funny* business', trickery, fraud; Godfrey Irwin and, hesitantly, *The O.E.D. Supplement*, (*tele*)*phone* or (*tele*)*phoney*; and, with less authority *Forney*, reputedly a late nineteenth-early twentieth century New York merchant, specializing in cheap or imitation jewellery. All three etymologies are both anachronistic and inadequate. The phonetic and semantic development would seem to be:

Irish *fainne*, a finger ring; approximate pronunciation, *fawney*.

5*

English cant (or underworld) *fawney* or *fawny*, a ring used in the *fawney rig* (1781) or ring-dropping game for the deception of the unwary, the practiser being a *fawney rigger* (1781). Irish confidence tricksters came to London quite early.

American cant *fawney*, in the same sense: adopted from England before 1851 (E. Z. C. Judson, *The Mysteries of New York*) and still current in 1906 (A. H. Lewis, *Confessions of a Detective*) and later.

American *fawney man*, a peddler of imitation jewellery; Josiah Flynt, article 'The American Tramp' in *The Contemporary Review*, August 1891—memories of 'the road' valid for at least a decade before 1890.

American *phoney* (or *phony*) *guy*, variant of the preceding term: from before 1905, Owen Kildare, *The Wisdom of the Simple*.

Phoney man, still in this 'peddler' sense: recorded in 1931, but used at least as early as 1910.

American *phoney stiff*, in same sense: from before 1918, Leon Livingston, *Madame Delcassee of the Hobos*.

Two phonetic and semantic links: 1828, Pierce Egan, *Finish to the Adventures of Tom, Jerry, and Logic*. 'He sports a diamond *forney* on his little finger'—compare *Forney* the jeweller; 1912, Donald Lowrie, *My Life in Prison*, 'There is a phoney note in his voice'.

And those are merely the highlights of the evidence for the etymology I tersely proposed in *A Dictionary of Slang*, fifteen years ago.

(Written in August 1952.)

BABES, BABBLERS, BARBARIANS

THESE three classes of potential humans share two qualities, if they can be called qualities: indistinct speech and constant speaking, if they can be called speech and speaking: all three are primitives. The barbarians emerge as by far the worthiest of the three classes, for they merely seem to babble and be indistinct; they suffer from the shocking disadvantage of not being those who dub them barbarians. In the speech of all three classes the element of stammering is implicit; in the naming, it is explicit for babblers and barbarians.

We, however, are concerned rather with the names than with the physiological and social facts. The basic words are *babe*, not the diminutive *baby*; 'to *babble*'; and *barbarous* or perhaps rather its Greek original, *barbaros*.

Babe and therefore *baby* are—like the related Swedish dialectal *babbe*, a child, Albanian *bebe* and Cornish and Welsh *baban*, a baby, Middle High German *buobe* (German *Bube*), a boy— formed in imitation of a baby's cries, much as *papa* and *mama* were originally childish names for the parents. Obviously these words are akin to Greek *babazo* (stem *babaz-*, root *bab-*), I prattle. To *babble* (Middle English *bablen*) is no less echoic than the related Swedish *babbla*, Norwegian *bable*, Ger *babbeln*, Dutch *babbelen* (cf. French *babiller*), to prattle; compare Latin *babulus*, a babbler, and the cognate L *balbare*, less usual than *balbutire*, to stammer (OHG *balbzōn*), the adjective *balbus*, stammering, whence the Proper Name *Balbus*, and Sanskrit *balbūthás*, a stammerer, *balbalá-karoti*, he stammers; a nasal variant appears in the Gr *bambainō*, I stammer, with which compare the Italian *bambino*, child, a diminutive of *bambo*, childish, from *bambalo*, a child, itself from L *bambalo*, stammerer. ('Babe' Ruth, the American baseball star of yesteryear, was nicknamed 'The Bambino'.)

Sanskrit *balbūthás*, stammerer (used as a man's name), is intimately akin to the synonymous Skt *barbaras*, itself clearly aligned with Gr *barbaros*, whence L *barbarus*, whence *barbarous*. (Compare the Celtic deviations in Gaelic *borb*, barbarous, and Old Irish *borp*, foolish.) The Greeks used the plural *barbaroi* of all non-Greeks; the Romans applied *barbari* to all non-Romans and, if they were in a good humour, also to those who were neither Italic nor Greek—in short, to barbarians. To the Greeks, *barbaroi* meant foreigners, originally stammerers or gabblers, the speakers of an unintelligible foreign language, consisting apparently of meaningless sounds and frequent repetitions of striking syllables, caused either by stammering or by childishness.

Now, it is insufficient to say, as a usually trustworthy and often enlightening authority says, that Gr *barbaros* probably comes from (an assumed) *barbar*, 'echoic word used for description of foreign tongues', a statement not so much incorrect as subtly misleading. *Barbaros* has stem *barbar-*, it is true; but *barbar-* (compare the Irish and Gaelic *barbar-*) follows a pattern or, if you prefer, belongs to an Indo-European group that, essentially reduplicative, has root *ba-*, with predominant stem *bal-*. The principal extensions and a few of the examples can perhaps be seen at their clearest in some such form as this:

bab-, as in L *babulus*, babbler, fool, L *babiger*, *baburrus*, Medieval L *babugus*, *babosus*, foolish, and the already mentioned Germanic cognates, whether of the *baby* or the *babble* type;

bal-, as in L *balbus*, stammering, Middle Irish *balb*, mute, stammering, Gaelic *balbh*, mute; reduplicated in L *Balbillus* (not merely a diminutive) and *balbutire*; with even clearer reduplication in Sanskrit *balbalas*, (variant of *barbaras*), *balbūthāls*, *balbalá-karoti*;

bam-, a nasalized form, in the reduplications *bambainō*, I chatter with the teeth, I stammer, and *bambakuzō*, *bambalizō* (or *-uzō*), my teeth chatter with cold, and, for a Slavic example, Lithuanian *bambeti*, to mumble or mutter;

bar-, reduplicated *barbar-*, as in Gr *barbaros*, the most striking example of all, even though *bal(bal)-*, much more frequent, exhibits such variants as the Russian *bolobóliti*, to gossip ramblingly, and the metathetic synonyms, or virtual synonyms, the

Bulgarian *blabolja* (or *blǎbolja*), the Serbian *blebetati*, the Lithuanian *blebenti*.

It should be noted that, in this complex group of words, there can scarcely have been anything like continuous derivation: several 'universal' experiences, inevitably and constantly renewed, have maintained the idea and revived the word in one form or another.

But do we find this sort of reduplication, this emphatic echoism, outside of Sanskrit and the European section of the Indo-European framework of languages? Persian possesses the word *tātār*: in the Middle Ages, Persians bestowed the name *Tātār* upon those Mongolian (and Turkic) tribesmen who invaded, first central and then western Asia and finally eastern Europe. Admittedly the word may have been of Tatar origin; it does, however, oddly and even remarkably insinuate itself into a receptive mind, as it did into geographer Lionel Lyde's, as probably an Iranian variation upon the *barbar* theme; to the Persians, the Mongolian and Turkic hordes were the new *barbarians* from the East. Even if from a Tatar source, the Persian *Tātār* has probably been influenced by the *barbar*-prototype. As not every schoolboy knows, the spelling *Tartar* is due to the influence of *Tartaros*, the ancient Greek nether-world—a word that, incidentally, the etymologists of Greek so very discreetly say nothing about, but is probably of Egyptian origin.

From the comparative uncertainty of that Persian word, let us pass to the irrefutable certainty of a Hebrew word. In Deuteronomy, ii, 20–21, we hear of 'a land of giants: giants dwelt therein in old time; and the Ammonites call them Zam-zummims; a people great, and many, and tall, as the Anakims; but the Lord destroyed them'. The Authorized Version's *s* at the end of the name is as unwarranted as that in the mongrel plural *seraphims*, *-im* being already the Hebrew plural. Now, *Zamzummim* has the clearly echoic triliteral root *zmm*. In Hebrew, as the Regius Professor of Hebrew at Cambridge generously tells me, this root signifies 'to consider, purpose, devise'; he adds that, 'in Arabic, which is more relevant here, it means "speak, talk", and another part of the verb, *zamzama*, the important reduplicated form for us in the present context, means "mumble, speak unclearly". So it would appear that to the Ammonites the speech they heard was just mumbling. A connection can, I believe, be found between the Hebrew and Arabic roots, for the Semite tends not to muse or ponder in silence, but vocally, in a mumbling, crooning sort of way.' All that remains to be said about this 'Hebrew parallel of the Greek *barbaroi*' is that a genuine nation or at least tribe, not a mythological race of giants, is intended.

Reduplication probably occurs in numerous other names of ancient peoples. An illuminating example of purest echoism is afforded by the Egyptian *aāā*, with 'extended' form *aāā-ta*, foreigner, barbarian. Something rather similar has occurred in the mid-nineteenth century New Zealand *Wee-Wees*, the French, in reference to the multiple *Oui, oui*'s of their conversation; a name paralleled by the Crimean War Tommies' *Deedonks*, in reference to the equally common *Dis donc!*, offset by the French soldiers' *I say* for a Tommy during the same campaign. The most famous of such terms is the Late Medieval French name for an Englishman: *godon*, from the national oath, *God damn!*: unless this be a particularly tenacious example of folk-etymology, as I suspect.

Folk-etymology may have entered into one or two other words mentioned above.

THE ETYMOLOGY OF *ETYMOLOGY*

THE etymology of every compound word falls into three very
unequal parts: the etymology of the compound as such; the
connective; the etymology of the separate elements, normally
two, as here. In a dictionary, the first stage is rightly the only
one treated in full: the connective is sometimes indicated; the
separate elements are usually, and should be always, shown
clearly, mostly in the form they have assumed in English, with
perhaps a parenthetical reference to the original.

Etymology, for instance, comes from Old French *ethimologie*,
Modern *étymologie*—already in Old French was *th* pronounced
t—from Latin *etymologia*, a mere approximate transliteration of
Greek *etumologia* (ἐτυμολογία), itself an abstract noun formed
from *etumologos* (ἐτυμολόγος), an etymologist, compounding
etumon (our *etymon*), the true thing, strictly the neuter of *etumos*,
true, and -*logos*, one who discourses, and consisting of the basic
etum-+the connective -*o*- +-*logos*, discourser. This -*logos* exists
only as a compound-forming element and is therefore not to be
confused with, although obviously it is very intimately related
to, *logos*, word. Perhaps, however, it would be more accurate to
say that the -*logos* of *etumologos* derives from *logos*, word, speech,
discourse, no less directly than does the combining-form -*logia*
present in *etumologia*. *Etymology*, therefore, is a discourse on the
true: that is, on the true origin of a particular word or of words
in general. Compare Cicero's attempt to Latinize *etumologia*:
ueriloquium, a speaking about the true, and, not only semantically, the English *soothsaying* and *soothsayer*.

Since the Greek *etumologia* represents *etum* (on)+-*o*-+-*logia*,
the connective is -*o*-, which occurs even more often in Greek
than -*i*- does in Latin; but then, Latin has, in numerous
learnèd words, adopted the Greek connective. This -*o*- is
attached to the stem—to the oblique stem if there be one—of
the first element. *Etumos* has stem *etum*-, hence *etum-o-logia*, our
etym-o-logy; *larunx* (λάρυγξ), our *larynx*, has oblique stem *larung*-

(λάρυγγ-, the genitive being λάρυγγος), our *laryng-*; hence our *laryng-o-logy*. Some day a scholar more erudite than myself will write a paper on connectives in Greek, Latin, one of the Romance languages, preferably French, and one of the Germanic languages, preferably English. The theme of connectives is linked with that of compound-forming elements. But the latter theme deserves an entire thesis, or, better, a mature study.

Thus we come to the two separate elements of *etymology*: *etym-*, standing for *etymon*, and *-logy*, standing for the abstract, or the collective, of *logos*. Both belong to fundamental words or, rather, word-groups, and both, therefore, deal with fundamental ideas: the idea of 'the *true*', truth, and that of 'to speak', speech, words, discourse.

Etymon refers to a complete word, in contradistinction to both *stem* or *theme* and to *root* or *radical*; the latter refers to the irreducible core of a word, especially to the Indo-European base of that word. We may, however, speak of the (Old) English stem, the French stem, the Latin stem, the Greek stem, the Sanskrit stem, and so forth, largely because the stems are usually known, whereas the Indo-European root is hypothetical.

Etymon has been adopted from Latin, which thus transliterated Greek *etumon* (ἔτυμον), noun, originally the neuter singular of the adjective *etumos* (ἔτυμος), true, with stem *etum-*; compare *ta etuma* (τὰ ἔτυμα), the true (things), truths, hence, collectively, truth. *Etumos* forms an extension or elaboration of *eteos* (ἐτεός), true, (originally) real, stem *ete-* or *eta-*. But *eteos* appears to vary the synonymous *etos* (ἐτός), which, recorded in the feminine singular *eta* (ἐτά), in the senses 'true' and 'good', has the root *et-*, whence also *etazō* (ἐτάξω), I verify. According to the late and much-lamented Belgian scholar Emile Boisacq, corroborating Brugmann, who was corroborating Curtius, *etos*, good, true, real—good because true, true because real— descends from an Indo-European root *set(o)-*, parallel to *sot(o)-*. Whereas the *s-* and the *e-* of *seto* recur in Greek *esti* (ἔστι), he is, the *s-* and the *-o-* of *sot(o)-* appear in *hosios* (ὅσιος), just, permissible, and also in Old English *sōth*, true, whence the Modern *sooth*, adjective hence noun, surviving only in the archaic *in good sooth* and *sooth to say* or *tell* and in *sooth-sayer*, *-saying*, a speaker, a speaking, of the truth. This Indo-European group presents problems and complexities. One of these features is easily explainable: Greek exhibits a constant tendency, initiated probably in Ionian and perhaps also in Lesbian Greek, to substitute a rough breathing for a smooth—or, in other words, to de-aspirate, e.g. in *etos* and *sooth* as compared with *hosios*. This process affords one manifestation of what is known to philologists as Psilosis, from *psiloun*, to strip. Belonging to this constellation, however, are several forms germane to its scope and nature; especially the Sanskrit *satya*, true, just, *satyám*, truth, and notably *sat*, *sant*, *san*, real, existent, strictly a present participle from a verb-root **as-* or **es-*, meaning 'to be', as in Sanskrit *asti*, Latin *esse*, the latter word reminding us of Greek *esti*, Latin (and French) *est*, English *is*. The nasalization exemplified by Sanskrit *sant*, *san*, is seen also in Old Norse *sannr*, true, from Primitive Germanic **santh(a)-*, and in Gothic *sunjis* (*j* pronounced as *y*), true, *sunja*, truth, from Primitive Germanic **sunja-*, itself from **sundia-*, answering, as Boisacq notes, to Sanskrit *satyá-*; and again in Old High German *sand*, real; compare the *sent-* of the Latin oblique stems *absent-* and *present-* (our *absent* and *present*) and, without the initial *s*, the Doric *entes* (ἔντες), originally a plural of the present participle, hence a plural noun.

The hypothetical Indo-European root and stems and their recorded ancient manifestations bear, it is easy to see, the basic sense 'to exist, to be', hence 'to be real'; the derivative nouns and adjectives accordingly bear the senses 'reality', hence 'truth' (and pragmatically 'goodness'), and 'real', hence 'true' (and 'good'). The predominantly Germanic *true*, on the other hand, proceeds rather from the fundamental concept of 'faithful' or 'loyal', as in 'a *true* friend'. As the Greek concept underlying *etos*, *eteos*, *etumos*, began by being, as to some extent it remained, realistic, practical, yet good-sensible, and ended by being intellectual, so the Germanic concept enshrined in *true*, *truth*, began by being, as appreciably it remained, common-sensible, practical, became social, and ended by being ethical and somewhat emotional. At least, that is in the main valid;

the differentiation must not be carried beyond the discernible.

From that brief and pathetically inadequate inspection of the birth and blood-relations of *etymon*, we pass to the second element of *etymology*; that is, to -*logy*. Now, -*logy* has a family tree that might be traced thus:

Modern English -*logy*;
(Early Modern English, especially English Renaissance, -*logie*);

Old French -*logie*, naturally applying only where the English word does not come from Latin or Greek or has not been formed directly thereon;

Latin -*logia*, when not by-passing that language;
Greek-λόγια, -*logia*;
Greek (λόγος, *logos*, word, account (whether narrative or commercial), discourse;
Greek λέγω, *legō*-, originally 'I assemble, I gather, I select', hence 'I enumerate' and especially 'I say, I speak'. Akin to Greek *legō*-, stem *leg*-, are:
Latin *legō*, I gather, and *elegans*, '(one who) picks out, hence discriminates, has good taste'—hence 'elegant'; and *legio*, whence our *legion*, a body of levies, chosen troops;
Greek λέξις, *lexis*, a word spoken or written, a phrase, diction, and λογίζομαι, *logizomai*, I count or calculate.

Note that whereas Greek *legō*, I gather, becomes *legō*, I say or speak, Latin *legō*, I gather, becomes *legō*, I read: speech is a choice of words to say, reading a choice of words to consider. (Note also that *logos* has the derivative sense 'reason', as in *logic*, the art of reasoning. One can think clearly, therefore reason well, only by wisely gathering and carefully choosing one's words.) Both the Greek and the Latin words display the priority of the Greek and Latin stem *leg*- over the Greek stem *log*- and the Latin stem *loq*- (*loqui*, to speak). The latter permits us to see that Latin *leg*- and *loq*- cover a wider semantic field— a wider range of ideas—than do the Greek *leg*- and *log*-; yet we must add the caution that no relevant Latin word is invested with the richness and profundity of meaning and association we find in the Greek *logos*, wherein word becomes thought becomes reason and, as *Logos* in New Testament Greek, the potently active, the creative, the revelatory thought, hence will, of God : 'In the beginning was the Word [λόγος], and the Word was with God, and the Word was God' (καὶ θεὸς ἦν ὁ λόγος).

To return to the derivative Greek *-logia*, English *-logy*, we notice that both the single, particular meaning, and the collective, general meaning of *logos*, 'word, a speaking' and 'discourse', hence 'treatise', even 'theory', are reflected in English no less than in Greek compounds, the former in, e.g., *tautology* and the latter in, e.g., *zoology*. *Etymology* itself is both particular as to a single word and collective as to one language or all languages; it may express itself in a specific quest or in general research. If, in some respects, etymology is a science in the modern sense, it is also a science in the old sense. Its exercise and methods are those of a science, of all science, but also those of an art, all art.

Etymology, ἐτυμολογία, is therefore etymologically, as well as by definition, a discourse on the true word, the real word, the original word, hence on the truth of words collectively, especially on the true origins embedded in the reality of words. Etymology, in short, forms the philological aspect of the philosophical problem of truth and of mankind's search for truth.

Note. The sign * before a word indicates an assumed form.

WHENCE *HOGMANAY*?

Hogmanay, December 31 and notably the evening thereof—a gift made, especially to children, on that day—children's cries of eager demand for or of gratified reception of that gift, hence the joyous celebration of the joyous occasion—this *Hogmanay* (strictly, capitalled only in the calendar sense) has caused, I was going to say more trouble than enough, but that would not be true, for it is the word, not the occasion, which has caused all the trouble among the etymologists in particular, the philologists in general, and among those inquiring laymen (bless 'em) who make the etymologist's life worth living, those unpretentious word-lovers who are welcomed by every true wordman.

In view of the bitter controversies it has caused, we do well to recall that *Hogmanay* was earliest recorded in the following shapes: *Hogmynae, ca.* 1680; *Hagmane*, 1693; *Hagmana*, 1694; *Hagman Heigh, Hagmenay, Hagmenai*, all in 1790; *Hogmanay*, 1792. The variation *hog-, hag-*, may be important and is certainly not to be ignored.

The most reputed etymologists have disposed thus of *Hogmanay: The Oxford English Dictionary* says 'Of obscure history', makes some valuable comments on earlier theories, and suggests an origin in a dialectal variation of the Old French *aguilanneuf*, New Year's Day, new year's gift; *Webster's New International Dictionary* gives a 'perhaps' support to Oxford's suggestion, which, by the way, owes much to Joseph Wright's proposal in *The English Dialect Dictionary*; and Ernest Weekley, in the 1952 edition of *A Concise Etymological Dictionary of Modern English*, flatly declares, 'Origin unknown'. All three are agreed that the word has not a Celtic origin.

The guesses concerning the origin are so disparate, the material so incongruous and even inconsequent, that, to avoid drowning in a welter of turbulent cross-currents, one is forced to conclude that the simplest way of dealing with the proposed etymologies and of arriving perhaps at a plausible and, pending further evidence, provisional solution, is to ignore the most glaring absurdities and divide the theories into the two main classes: already propounded; only now propounded. The former includes two patently improbable origins, the one in Greek, the other in Spanish, and two French origins, the one all-explanatory but folk-etymological, the other explanatory only in part, but scholarly, and one excellent Latin suggestion; the latter consists of an improbable French and a suggestive Latin origin.

The Greek origin was first put forward in 1694, by Robert Calder in *Scotch Presbyterian Eloquence Display'd*, where he says 'It is ordinary among some plebeians to go about from door to door upon New Year's eve, crying Hagmana, a corrupted word from the Greek Hagia-mana, which signifies the holy month'. Calder probably intends the second element of his Greek word to be phonetic, the usual transliteration being *hagia mēnē* (ἅγια μήνη). One need hardly prove the ineligibility of this guess: to equate an entire month to one day seems, to put it mildly, absurd.

The Spanish guess is of the same low order. The Spanish equivalent, *aguilando* (now *aguinaldo*), has been derived from Latin *calendae*, the first day of the Roman month: but the Spanish probably came from the French and can hardly have originated *hogmanay*. As for the French variant *aguilanleu* and the aphetic *guilanlé* being derived from *calendae*, well . . . !

Of the two French origins already proposed, let us glance at the improbable before passing to the quite probable theory. Even the improbable one has several variants. John Jamieson, in his *An Etymological Dictionary of the Scottish Language*, revised edition, 1880, quotes an anonymous late eighteenth-century philologist as citing a beggars' call '*Au gui menez*, Roi Follet' and a Gaulish Druidic chant '*Au gui l'an neuf*, le Roi vient' and an Aquitaine custom associated with December 31 and emphasizing the cry *Au guy! l'an neuf!*—'To the mistletoe, the New Year [comes]!' The O.E.D. has shown the first to be a figment of the imagination and remarked that 'these' and one or two similar 'explanations, with the reference to the *gui* or mistletoe, are now rejected by French scholars as merely "popular ety-mology".'

The O.E.D., however, notes that '*Hogmanay* corresponds exactly in sense and use to Old French *aguilanneuf*'. The form *aguilanneuf* occurs as primary in Godefroy's dictionary of Old French, which gives such variants as *aguillanneuf, aguilleneuf, aguilleneu, aguilanleu, aguillenleu,* and the significant *haguilennef* and *haguirenleu*. Godefroy cites also such dialectal forms as the truncated *aguilan* and the aphetic *guilané* and *guilanneu*. *Aguil(l)-anneuf* does not occur until 1480; all the early forms end in -*u* or in -*o*; -*f* is probably a learned refashioning.

The *lanneuf* part of *aguil(l)anneuf*, if we accept it, seems clear and constant; it very probably represents *l'an neuf,* the new year, the New Year. 'Although the phonetic difference between *aguillanneuf* and the Scotch word is great, the Norman form *hoguinané* is much closer to *hagmané, hogmanay,* and it cannot be doubted that both the custom and the term are from the French' (O.E.D.). *Webster* accepts all this; and Joseph Wright's etymology in *The English Dialect Dictionary* antedates and supple-ments the O.E.D., thus: 'Of French origin. Compare Norman dialectal *hoquinano, haguinelo,* cries on New Year's Eve; *hoguilan-no* (at Caen), a New Year's gift.'

These three great authorities imply a belief in the validity of the '*lanneuf* (*lanneu,* etc.)=the New Year' solution. Perhaps wisely, they avoid saying anything of the first element *agui* or *hagui,* or *hogui* or *hoqui*. Before dealing with the theory I myself rather fancy, I mention, most apologetically, a momentary idea that came to me: that such forms as *hoguinane, hoquinano,* might possibly point to an origin in *houp à l'an neuf,* which, *houp* being an echoic term (roughly equivalent to *whoop*), might be colloquially translated 'whoops for the New Year!' That, how-ever, is folk-etymology.

Here is a serious proposal.

As we have noticed, the first element of *aguilanneuf,* etc., is *agui-* or *hagui-* on the one hand and, on the other, *hogui-* or *hoqui-*. These may be combining-forms of the stems *ag-* or, aspirated, *hag-* and of *hog-* or *hoq-*. We may, I think, discard the unaspirated *ag-*: the French dislike aspirates. The conflict between *hag-* and *hog-* (or *hoq-*) would disappear if we accepted the supposition that Old French derives the *hag-* forms from the cry:

haec [dona] *anno novo*, these gifts for the New Year; and the *hog-* (*hoq-*) forms from the alternative or variant cry:

hoc [donum] *anno novo*, this gift for the New Year. The terminal *g* is merely a thickening of terminal *c*; *hoq-* a mere variant of *hoc-*.

Anyone who knows anything about French, knows that *an neuf* derives, singly and jointly, from Latin *annus novus* (*novus*; not the Classical Latin *nouus*), the new year. The Norman dialectal forms *hoquinano* and *hogilanno* are very important: the latter shows the influence of the *aguilanneuf-haguilennef* type (with medial *l*, probably the *l'* of the French 'the') and both, with their -*an(n)o* ending, indicate at least a possibility of origin either based on or influenced by the Latin dative *anno novo*, for the new year, as we saw it used above in

haec [dona] *anno novo*,

whence the *hag-*, *haq-* derivatives, and in

hoc [donum] *anno novo*,

whence the *hog-*, *hoq-* derivatives. There has been an intimate interaction between the Latin *annus novus* and *anno novo* and the French *l'an neuf*. The exact nature and the precise order of such interactions are sometimes impossible to unravel.

That Latin origin may, by some, be preferred to W. W. Skeat's. In his still invaluable work, *An Etymological Dictionary of the English Language*, 4th edition, 1910, Skeat includes *hogmanay* in the supplement and closely follows the etymology proposed in 1849 by A. Duméril in *Dictionnaire du Patois Normand*, where, on the evidence of a noted seventeenth-century scholar, Jacques Moisant de Brieux, is quoted an old song, bearing the refrain *hoquinano* (with variant *haquinelo*). Duméril interprets *hoquinano* as *hoc in anno*, in this year. Phonetically that interpretation is faultless, especially as *hoquinano* could so easily become *hoquinane*, and *hoquinane* become *hoguinane*, which, as Skeat says, would ultimately account for *hogmanay*. The sense,

however, is inferior. My proposal of *hoc* (donum) *anno novo*, this
gift for the New Year, yields better sense; and *hoc anno novo*
could develop thus:

> *hocannonovo*
> *hoc'nono; -vo* being naturally dropped
> *hocnano*
> *hognano*
> *hogmano*
> *hogmané*
> *hogmanay.*

On that genial note, I bid such readers as have endured to
the end: a bonny *hogmanay* and a happy New Year's Eve and
New Year's Day.

AN AMERICAN HALF-DOZEN

OF the various American words imported by Britain from late 1939 onwards, six have that particular interest which comes from a not immediately obvious etymology or word-history. In the order of their importation, these are: *phoney; goon; G.I.; jeep; jaloppy;* and *malarkey* (or *-ky*) or, in a variant pronunciation, *malakky*. *Phoney* reached us during the Autumn of 1939, in the phrase 'the phoney war', applied by Americans to the static warfare of those deceptive days; *goon*, a little later, from an American cartoon. *Jeep* and *G.I.* arrived in 1942, a direct result of American participation in a war become notably less 'phoney'. *Jaloppy* infiltrated, during 1950, by way of the cinema, and *malarkey*, through the same medium, was by late 1951 only just beginning to be known in Britain.

The first five terms will be found in the most recent editions of *Webster*, and of *Funk and Wagnalls*, and in Mitford Mathews's *Dictionary of Americanisms* (April 1951), but *malarkey* appears neither in these three dictionaries nor in the *American College Dictionary*. Whereas *jaloppy* is uniformly said to be 'of unknown, or obscure, origin', *phoney* is mostly explained incorrectly. But *goon*, *G.I.*, and *jeep* have been tolerably well treated.

In America, *phoney*, often written *phony*, has usually been derived either from tele*phoney*, on the ground that it is so much easier to tell lies over the telephone than it is to do so when face to face with one's intended dupe, or from *funny*—on the analogy of *funny business*, trickery, dishonesty; or again, from an American jeweller named *Forney*, who specialized in 'imitation'. Naturally enough, Americans tend to prefer an American origin. The evidence, however, points to *phoney*'s being an American variation of an English word. The twentieth century American underworld term *phoney stiff*, a vagrant or any other peddler of imitation jewellery, should have indicated where the origin might be discovered, for earlier—the 1880's and 1890's— it had occurred as *fawney man*, for instance in Josiah Flynt's once famous work *Tramping with Tramps*, 1899. Compare the English underworld's *fawney cove*, recorded in 1848 and probably current from long before that date. As early as 1781, the ring-dropping game, one of the old everlastings for fooling the credulous, was known as *the fawney rig*, the fawney trick, *fawney* being an English attempt at the Irish *fainné*, a finger ring. That evidence should suffice, even for those philologists who are reluctant to accept any explanation not made by themselves.

For *goon*, however, I suggested, in my *Dictionary of the Underworld*, a wrong etymology—*goof* and *coon*, by the process of blending. But the original American sense—a 'strong arm man', a thug—should have put me on the right track; and, indeed, *Webster* explains *goon* correctly as having been adopted from a comic strip by the ingenious cartoonist E. C. Segar, who, the creator of Popeye and other delightful creatures, died in 1938. Segar invented the *Goons*, a sub-human race, and derived the name 'probably from *goo*rilla and bab*oon*'. Among British prisoners of war in Germany or in German-controlled Italy, *goon* humorously denoted a German guard or sentry. Segar's goons had been known, from before the war, to many Britons; but the term *goon* was hardly used by them before 1940.

Then, in 1942—if not already in 1941—came *jeep*, and, in 1942, *G.I.* By 1945 or 1946 one of the most widely distributed terms in the world, *jeep* likewise derives from a Segar comic strip. *Popeye* contained a wonder worker, a rat-like creature named Eugene, whose chief contribution to the world's speech consisted of the sound *jeep*. Hardly less of a wonder worker, as those who know it well are the first to proclaim, was the American utility van—or—'multipurpose cross-country vehicle' as Webster defines it—which, precisely because it was a *g*eneral *p*urpose, or *G.P.*, vehicle, came to be associated with the *jeep*-uttering Eugene. This is *Webster's* etymology: and it has been endorsed by Professor John W. Clark, a far from gullible person, in his (and my) *British and American English since 1900*.

One of the American Army rank and file, especially a private, was a *G.I.* or, among Americans, a *G.I. Joe*, the *Joe* merely humanizing the reference. This sense of *G.I.*, declared 'illegal' by the Department of War, derives from the equally slangy adjectival use, as in '*G.I.* haircut'—according to regulations; and the latter sense derives from the quartermaster's use, technical, not slangy, as in 'a pair of *G.I.* shoes' or 'a *G.I.* cap'—that is, shoes or cap from government *i*ssue, which, throughout the army, was, of course, general *i*ssue. The soldier, himself almost as expendable as anything he wore or carried, owes the nickname to a blend of the ideas in *G.I.*; he was both general issue and government issue. Clearly, then, *G.I.* is semantically comparable to *jeep*. (In the art and science of etymology, semantics has reference to ideas rather than to forms.)

With both *jaloppy* and *malarkey*, we are upon uncharted seas. *Jaloppy*—pronounced jă-lop'-ĭ even when the word is written *jalopy*—meaning usually a dilapidated or very old-fashioned car, and, occasionally, a similarly decrepit or outmoded aircraft, was first recorded in the middle 1920's as current in Chicago, at that time gangster-ridden, and the centre of the stolen-car racket. The earliest spelling is *jaloppi*. That spelling makes me wonder whether *jaloppy* were originally an Italian gangster's distortion of *jalapy*, the rather colloquial adjective of *jalap*, a very widely used purgative. The predominant connotation of *jaloppy* could well be 'messy': hence, such a car would be thought of as 'a mess'. In support of this supposition, we have *heap*. In the *American Mercury* of May 1929, Ernest Booth has written: '*Heap* is fairly recent, about eight or ten years old. Its origin is obvious: Automobile = heap of junk = any machine.' *Heap*, first an underworld term, would obviously have been known to the Chicago gangsters. The semantic link between *heap* and *jaloppy* is almost offensively apparent.

Malarkey (or -*ky*), pronounced mă-lar'-kĭ—or *malakky* (or -*ey*), pronounced mă-lak'-kĭ—roughly means 'deliberately misleading talk'; 'the tale'; 'soft soap'. It occurs in such a sentence as: 'Don't give me the old malarkey', where *malarkey* is almost synonymous with the hardly less slangy *run-around*. The *soft soap* nuance—compare the obsolescent *soft sawder*—affords an exciting clue. In scientific terminology, there exists the combining element *malaco-* or, before a vowel, *malac-*, denoting or, at the least, connoting 'soft'. I remember enough Classical

Greek to recall that *malakós* means soft, and that its derivative noun *malakía* therefore means softness. But the sort of American who originated and gave currency to *malark(e)y* or *malakk(e)y* manifestly knew no Classical Greek—at least, as such. But Chicago, perhaps, and New York, certainly, contain as many Greeks as there are in Athens. The next question is: Does Modern Greek retain *malakós* and, pertinently, *malakía*? Modern Greek retains *malakós*, soft, and such derivatives as *maláka*, softening of the brain, and *malakótas*, softness, and *malakúnō*, I soften; it also retains *malakía*, but only in an unpleasant physiological sense, inapplicable here. What variants there may be in Modern Greek dialects, including those spoken in the United States, I cannot say. Yet there would seem to be, hypothetically, a pretty good case for deriving *malark(e)y*, *malakk(e)y*, from some modern form, or from some modern subsidiary, of either *malakós*, soft, or, more probably, *malakía*, softness.

The etymologies of *jaloppy* and *malarkey* are provisional; that of *phoney*, so nearly certain that I'd wager on it; that of *goon*, almost as likely; those of *G.I.* and *jeep*, very widely accepted and, presumably, correct.

(Published in *Truth*, September 28, 1951.)

ELEPHANTINE

UNTIL the twentieth century, the word *elephant* had the etymologists almost completely baffled; then, after several false starts, the second element of this compound was satisfactorily explained; the first element has caused much recrimination and still more doubt, even Professor C. D. Buck daring only a 'first part disputed'; and no whole-hearted attempt has been made to account either for the sense of the word as a whole or for the fact, or even the reason, of the compounding.

There have, in historic times, existed two kinds of elephant, the African and the Asian, the latter confined to the south; in Pleistocene times—the early Ice Age—elephants had roamed all regions except the polar and those of Australia and South America. We should historically expect to find *elephant* to be Indo-European or Semitic or Hamitic, rather than, say, Burmese: and, in the fact, the source is neither Burmese nor Malayan nor Chinese. But no more is it indigenously Sanskrit (*ibha-*, *ibhas, being, moreover, unrecorded before the Christian era) or indigenously Iranian (Old Persian *pīru-* being an adoption from Akkadian). The Sanskrit word—there's nothing resembling it in Dravidian—was probably imported into India by Arabs trading from Egypt or perhaps Ethiopia.

Let us work backwards. English *elephant* comes, through late Middle English *elephaunt, elefaunt*, from Old French *elefant*; the ME variants *olifaunt (-phaunt), -fante*, etc., derive from the OF variant *olifant*, presumably from a Vulgar Latin *oliphantus or *-fantus*, a form that seems to have influenced several Germanic languages. OF *elefant*, like VL *elephantus, derives from Latin *elephantus* (genitive *elephanti*), formed apparently from Greek *elephantos*, genitive of *elephas*, whence literary Latin *elephas* (gen. *elephantis*).

Greek ἐλέφας, *elephas*, occurs as 'elephant' in Herodotus (fifth century B.C.); in Homer (tenth B.C.) and Hesiod (eighth) it had meant 'ivory'. Herodotus perhaps apprehended *elephas* o be 'the *ivory* animal': certainly none of these three Greeks perceived that here was an obscure compound.

Of that compound, two very early forms[1] have been discovered—a Mycenaean Greek and a Hieroglyphic Hittite. The former, of about 1400 B.C., is *erepatejo* (an imperfect representation of Gr *elephanteios*), 'of ivory'; the latter is *ulubandas* or *ulupantas*, 'a bull' or 'a wild ox'. In very ancient times, the word for 'elephant' was sometimes used rather vaguely of any large (and strange?) quadruped: compare the confusion, in northern and north-eastern Europe, between the elephant and the camel, and the application of the former's name to the latter.

Of this vexing compound, the second element is E -*ephant*, OF -*efant*, L -*ephantus*, literary -*ephas*, Gr -*ephas* (-έφας), with oblique stem -*ephant*-: compare the Hittite -*upantas* (or -*ubandas*); compare also the Sanskrit *ibhas* and, 'ivory' only, the L *ebur* (oblique *ebor*-). Most scholars now hold that the origin of these Gr, L, Skt words lies in the Egyptian *abu* (variant *ab*), elephant, ivory, of which the synonymous Coptic is *ebu* (or *ebou*). Allowance being made for the shadowy, tentative, problematic vocalization of Eg *ab*, *abu*, one may fairly deduce that both Sanskrit *ibhas* and Hebrew shen*hab*im (ivory) are loan-words from Egyptian. L *ebur*, ivory, is particularly interesting: its nominative ending -*ur* and its oblique stem *ebor*- follow the pattern of L *robur*, oblique stem *robor*-; it probably came into Latin during, or soon after, Hannibal's invasion of Italy and therefore its form *eb*- (not Eg *ab*-) may have owed something to that late Phoenician (a Semitic language) known as Carthaginian; it certainly, as opposed to *elephantus*, owes nothing to Greek; and, through the L adjective *eboreus*, ivorine, and the derivative Old Fr noun *ivorie*, it constitutes the origin of *ivory* and, through the secondary L adjective *eburneus*, the literary *eburn*.

The first element has been more troublesome. It still is. This element is so predominantly *el*- that we should be wise to take *el*- as our base of operations. We do at least know that *el*- cannot, as many amateurs and a few professionals long believed or sug-

[1] Announced in articles published respectively by J. Chadwick, 1954, and by R. D. Barnett, 1948. I have simplified the transliterations.

gested, be the Arabic article 'the', for *l* (vocalized as *al* or *il* or especially *el*) did not antedate the Christian era. We can, moreover, be tolerably certain that *el-* is not a primitive Gr root *el-*, animal's horn (perhaps compare Gr *elaphos*, a stag), as several Continental scholars have proposed, because, momentarily seductive for Greek, it fails very badly in the comparative light of Semitic and Hamitic, which, by the way, exhibit one or two illuminating pointers to the ubiquity of the *l-r* alternation throughout not merely the Indo-European languages but also what I provisionally call 'Mediterranean' and Professor A. Cuny boldly calls 'Nostratique'.

The relevant Semitic words appear to be:

Assyrian-Babylonian, or Akkadian, *pīlu* or *pīru* (cf. the Old Persian *pīru-*) ;

Aramaic and Syriac *pīlā*; whence presumably

post-Biblical Hebrew *pīl*;

Arabic—and modern Persian—*fīl*;

perhaps the *fal-* of Ethiopic *falfal*, despite its meanings—'a fierce lion'—'a rhinoceros'—'a buffalo'.

(With Ar *fīl*, compare Old Norse *fill*, elephant, which came, probably by way of Russia, from some Semitic source, the likeliest being Arabic.)

Hamitic affords or appears to afford:

Tuareg (a Saharan Berber language) *elu*.

The Tuareg form is particularly significant, for it parallels so closely the Gr *el-*; yet the link could be illusory, not because it does not in fact exist but because one could build too much on it.

There are many factors to be considered, both of date and of form. The very division into two elements could lead us to postulate two entirely different words. There is a further complication in the meaning or meanings of the compound.

First: the compound *erapatejo* ('of ivory'—? originally, or also, 'of an elephant') belongs to the Mycenaean civilization of 1400–1100 B.C.; the compound *ulpantas* (or *ulbandas*) to that of the mainly Indo-European, ? partly Semitic, Hittite civilization of 1900–1200 B.C. Those joint facts justify us in postulating an IE origin of the compound. What, then, of the elements?

Could either of them be IE in origin? The second element, as we have seen, is very probably Hamitic; and the first element, if we rightly take *el-* to vary *il-*, and *il-* to be a worn-down form of Akkadian *pīlu*, is very probably Semitic, because Babylonian (the earliest form of Akkadian), which offers *pīlu* and its variant *pīru*, belongs to a civilization flourishing 2800–1700 B.C. and thus sets the existence of at least the first element at almost a millennium before that of the compound; nor is there any insuperable reason why the second element, especially in Egyptian, should not have been equally early.

Second: it is clear that if the Hittites and the Mycenaeans apprehended their compounds as consisting of two separate elements, i.e. originally two separate words, they must have thought of them—so far, we also have been thinking of them— as two words having different forms and presumably different meanings: each may have vaguely assumed that the name signified 'the *ivory* animal', for they could hardly have supposed them to signify 'the ivory elephant', much less 'the elephant-elephant'.

Yet 'the elephant-elephant' is precisely what the compound would probably have meant to an ancient Semite conversant with Hamitic or to an ancient Hamite conversant with Semitic, for the startling yet obvious reason that all the various Semitic and Hamitic names, whether very ancient or quite modern, spring from one single word common to the basic Semito-Hamitic stock. (One should never forget that the Egyptian civilization was highly developed by 3800 B.C., a date comparing well with that of the most ancient Semitic civilizations.) The brilliantly erudite Marcel Cohen is not alone in his belief that all the Semitic and Hamitic words for 'elephant' (and 'ivory', and both) were originally one word. This theory allows us to adduce several words that otherwise appear to hover between our postulated first element and our postulated second element—elements now seen to be ultimately identical—and those words are Galla *arba*, L *barrus* (hardly 'the carrier', as formerly believed but perhaps aphetic for *ebarrus*, itself for *eburrus*), and Gr *pirissas* (stem *piris-*, but root *pir-*), all meaning 'elephant' and all probably belonging to the *piru* group.

That all the relevant Semitic and Hamitic words preserved their meaning is a fact no less important than this other—that the original Semito-Hamitic form diverged early into two main groups, with perhaps a tiny third group (Gr and Tuareg *el-*), itself, nevertheless, better joined to either the *piru* or the Egyptian (-Coptic)-Sanskrit-?Hebrew group.

The Hittites and the Mycenaeans, ignorant of the Semito-Hamitic identity of the elements (if indeed they knew or even guessed their words to be compounds), would seem to have used, the latter in a presumably derivative adjective and the former in a noun that, despite the 'elephant'-'wild ox' confusion, is related, compounds consisting of two elements, deriving ultimately, the one from a Semitic and the other from a Hamitic word, themselves deriving from one common Semito-Hamitic name for a large quadruped most strikingly typified by the elephant. The explanation of *elephant* as semantically 'elephant-elephant' would thus cease to appear an absurdity. All IE languages with either a long history, as English has, or a very long history, as Greek has had, contain examples, few yet undeniable, of 'one-word tautology' or, better, 'semantic duplication'.

With pleasure and gratitude, I acknowledge debts to the following scholars: marginally, Professor H. Dubs, Dr Hla Pe, Sir R. Winstedt; on specific points, Professor T. Burrow, Professor W. B. Henning, Dr O. Szemerenyi; both specifically and generally—and most generously—Dr C. Rabin and Professor D. Winton Thomas. (All mistakes are, of course, mine, as also the choice of subject, the plan, the treatment.)

ASPECTS OF EMPTINESS

Starting from the basic idea 'empty', which implies the related idea 'emptied', Latin exhibits three words almost as clearly related in form as they are in sense. One of those Latin words has, or appears to have, a subsidiary; two of them have cognates in the Germanic languages; and both the Latin and the Old Germanic words are represented in modern English. The basic idea is so important, so pervasive, that it inevitably possesses various gradations or extensions or modifications or, in one word, aspects; that basic idea is expressed by a common root, with inevitable or almost inevitable variations of idea. It is well to remember that objects, hence objects-as-ideas, precede the words that pin-point and render generally available those ideas, hence those objects; the influence of words on ideas comes later—an influence that increases until we reach the absurdity of words being regarded as more important than ideas.

Here, we are dealing rather with ideas than with objects; obviously the ideas correspond to very important features of the physical world, but they are physical features and facts rather than objects. Language always lags behind reality, and always it is trying—sometimes quite desperately—to catch up, with the result that language is wasteful and reduplicatory: one clear initial idea had, initially, one clear word, although often the pundits fail to agree what that word was; the most important differentiations or developments—the principal aspects—acquire, each in its turn, a word that is, usually, a recognizable modification of the original word, but, human nature being inconsistent, ludicrously unsystematic, notoriously indiscriminatory, hopelessly repetitious, with the further result that each initially clear differentiated form, with its correspondingly differentiated sense, gathers to itself the subsidiary meanings, and even the initial meaning, of the other forms, and, as the senses get intermixed, so the forms tend to lose their sharp definition. Sounds are subject to the same or equivalent forces of change as senses are. The fashionable view is that all our ideas are confused; in the fact, it is words that, far more than ideas, tend to become confused—although, one hardly needs to add, ideas themselves are not free from that tendency. On balance and all things considered, those who have retreated from universal ideas to particular words, or indeed from ideas in general to words in general, have jumped from a precarious frying-pan into a perilous fire.

But let us bravely pass from the comparative comfort of philosophy to the hideous discomfort of philology and to the three aspects of emptiness. For the sake of convenience, the Medieval Latin (ML) initial *v-*, instead of the Latin (L) initial *u-*, is used throughout.

VACANCY

L *vacare*, to be empty, hence unoccupied, has present participle (presp) *vacans*, oblique stem (o/s) *vacant-*, and past participle (pp) *vacatus*, whence 'to *vacate*', the derivative *vacatio*, o/s *vacation-*, yielding *vacation*. *Vacare* has stem *vac-*, whence the adjective (adj) *vacuus*, whence *vacuitas*: E *vacuous* and *vacuity*. From *vacuus* comes *vacuare*, to rid (somebody) of (something), with compound *evacuare*, pp *evacuatus*, whence 'to *evacuate*', the derivative *evacuatio* giving us *evacuation*. The English nouns and adjectives have passed through French, as English nouns and adjectives derived from Latin mostly do.

L *vacuare* has the ancient variant *vocuare*, with frequentative *vocitare*, to empty often, used also as an intensive, to empty completely, whence the safely presumed Vulgar Latin adj *vocitus*: Old French-Medieval French (OF-MF) *vuit*, feminine *vuide*, dialectal variations *voit*, *voide*: English *void*. The subsidiary *avoid* and *devoid* have likewise reached us through OF-MF.

VANITY

L *vanus*, empty or emptied, hence without substance, hence vain, and its derivative *vanitas*, lead, through French, to *vain* and *vanity*. The original sense survives in 'All is vanity'. The off-shoots *vanescere*, to disappear, presp *vanescens*, the compound *evanescere*, and *vanitantes*, foolish people, finally produce 'to *vanish*', *evanescent*, 'to *vaunt*'; after French intervention.

Closely related to L *vanus* is L *inanis*, empty, our *inane*; *inanis* seems to have arisen as an intensive (denoted by *in-*) of *vanus*: probably *inanis* stands for *inanus*, itself for *inuanus*: *in-*+ *uanus* (our *vanus*). Derivative *inanitas* and *inanitio* become *inanity* and *inanition*.

Akin to L *vanus* are Old Norse (ON) *vanr*, Gothic (Go) *wans*, defective, the stem being that (*van-*) *wan-* which we see in Old English (OE) *wanian*, to be lacking or diminished, our 'to *wane*', and in Middle English (ME) *wantowen*, our *wanton*, the ME *-towen* representing OE *togen*, pp of *teon*, to draw or pull, hence to train: properly, *wanton* means 'deficient in training, hence in discipline'. The ON *vanr* has neuter *vant*, with verb *vanta*, to lack; hence our noun and, partly by inter-action, our verb *want*.

VASTNESS

The vast inane, which occurs more than once in seventeenth-century literature, is a phrase that puzzled my youth and now illuminates my theme. From the L *vastus*, deliberately ren-dered empty, i.e. ravaged or desolated, hence uncultivated, hence desert, hence, deserts being mostly large, very extensive, immense, comes *vast*. The compound *devastare* (*de-* is intensive), to lay utterly waste, has pp *devastatus* and derivative *devastatio*, o/s *devastation-*: 'to *devastate*' and *devastation*.

Akin to L *vastus* is OE *weste*, which has influenced the pas-sage of our adj *waste* (ME *wast*) from Old North French *wast*, a variant (*w-* for *gu-*: compare *ward* and *guard*) of OF-MF *guast*, itself from L *vastus*. The English noun and verb *waste* also derive from ONF. The somewhat baffling *wastrel*, origin-ally 'waste land', then 'an object wasted by inferior workman-ship', seems to have derived from 'to *waste*', with *-rel* perhaps borrowed from the even more baffling *scoundrel*, which has very probably influenced the modern sense (current hardly before 1840) of *wastrel*.

IN CONCLUSION (BUT INCONCLUSIVE)

We have, much too briefly, treated three L. words, *vacare*, with *vacuus*, *vacuare*—*vanus*, along with the synonymous *inanis*— and *vastus*, with *devastare*, and noted the Germanic cognates *wane* (*want*) and *waste*. We have noticed how confusingly, yet how naturally, their meanings overlap and interlock; how little (comparatively) their forms vary. To these words, we should add L *vascus*, empty, which, like the Greek and Celtic cognates, has been unproductive in English. Akin, especially to L *vanus* (*uanus*), are Sanskrit *unas*, defective, Gr *eunis*, deprived, Armenian *unain*, empty; akin, especially to L *uacare*, is Hittite *wakkar-*, to be lacking.

The Celtic cognates, even if (as some think) they do derive from Latin, are important, in that they illustrate the constant *ua-* (*va-*, *wa-*) and the variant extensions in *-c*, *-n*, *-s* (*-st*):

Cornish *gwag* (*guag*) or *gwak*, vacant, empty, vain: compare L *vac*uus;

Irish *faen*, weak, and Gaelic *faoin*, idle, trifling, silly, and Manx *feayn*, empty: compare L *van*us;

Old Irish *fas* (also Gaelic) or *faas*, empty, vacant, and Manx *faasagh* (adj), waste, desert, and probably Cornish *guastria*, to waste: compare L *vastus*.

For L *uanus*, *vascus*, *vastus*, the erudite Professors Ernout and Meillet postulate a root *uas-*, *was-*, empty; for *vacare*, they allow no more than *u-* as a common denominator. But certainly *ua-*, probably *uas-*, holds good for all four words. The inter-relationships can perhaps be shown or, at the least, implied in some such way as this:

root *uas-*, *was-*, *vas-*+extension *c*=*uasc-* (etc.), as in *uascus*, *vascus*; basic sense, 'empty';

uas-+*n*=*uasn-*, as in the presumed *uasnus*, whence *uanus*, *vanus*; basically, 'empty';

uas-+*t*=*uast-*, as in *uastus*, *vastus*; basically, 'empty'.

Moreover, the extension *uasc-* (as in *uascus*) perhaps had the presumed derivative *uascare*, to be empty, which might well have been eased to *uacare*, *vacare*.

In short, all these Latin words and their Old Germanic

cognates, as well as the Hittite *wakkar-* (root *wak-*), probably go back to an Indo-European *was-*, empty; and the Sanskrit, Greek, Armenian cognates of L *vanus* exhibit variations of that theme in its *uasn-* extension.

But this is a mere scratching of the surface.

... NOR ANY DROP TO DRINK

As air is life's *sine qua non*, water is its primary sustainer. The course of history has often been changed and occasionally it has been determined by the absence or insufficiency of water-supplies. On the material plane, therefore, the word for 'water' is probably the most widely distributed and, in many regions, perhaps the earliest coined of all.

Water itself and its cognates, whether certain or problematic, have a history so ancient, so rich, so complex, that only a very general, hence an exasperatingly inadequate, outline can be attempted here. (A less summary treatment will, circumstances permitting, appear in *Mediterranean*, itself a prolegomenon, due for publication in 1963.) Not all the groups or sub-groups are irrefutably cognate; each group, however, consists of words indisputably related one to another. Certain of the derivatives —for instance, *wash, eagre, osier, otter, hydra, dropsy*—are reluctantly omitted.

The five principal groups are sign-posted by *water*, along with *wet*; by *whisk(e)y*; by *undulate* and the perhaps unrelated *aqueous*; and by *hydrant*: respectively, yet only predominantly, Germanic, Celtic, Latin, Greek.

Existing already in Middle English, *water* has, through *weter*, come from Old English *waeter*, which possesses such Germanic cognates as Old Frisian *water*, variant *weter*, Old Saxon *watar*, early and modern Dutch *water*, Old High German *wazzar* (German *Wasser*), Gothic *watō*, with genitive *watins*, and Old Norse *vatn*; the *n* infix occurs also in, e.g., Lithuanian *vanduō*. Hittite, thought by some to be fully Indo-European and by others to be a sister language, exhibits *wātar*, variant *wetār*; a fact as easy to belittle as to exaggerate. With Old Norse *vatn*, water, compare ON *vāthr* or *vātr*, wet, and therefore OFris and Modern English *wet*, OE *wāet*, with all these forms, compare ON *vetr*, winter, and—with the *n* infix and with another change of vowel—the Dutch, OFris, Middle (and Modern)

167

High German, OE-ME-E *winter*, and OS and OHG *wintar*; the wet, or the rainy, season. In several Indo-European languages, the words for 'water' and 'rain' are, unsurprisingly, identical.

From the mainly Germanic we pass to the mainly Celtic, the key-word being *whisk(e)y*, owing its sense to Irish *uisgebeatha*, literally 'water of life', i.e. whiskey (contrast the French *eau-de-vie*, brandy), and its form to the Irish and Gaelic *uisge*, water, from Old Irish *uisce*, variant *usce*, apparently an extension of the Celtic root *au-* or *av-*, water. Compare the Welsh-Cornish-Breton *avon*, a river, with the Cornish variant *awan* and the Manx *awin*; the Irish and Gaelic forms have *b* instead of *u* or *v* or *w*; the importance of these Celtic words will emerge later, their undisputed kinship being to Latin *aqua*, not to Latin *unda*.

'To *undulate*' derives, ultimately, from *unda*, a wave, hence also water, akin to Sanskrit *udan-* (genitive *udnas*); it forms a nasalized cognate of Greek *hudōr*, water, whence, somewhat irregularly, the English *hydrant* and, regularly from a compound, *hydraulic*; *hudatos*, the Greek genitive, helps us to see the relationship of *hudor* to *water*. *Unda*, a wave, is easily visible in *inundate*, soon perceived in *redundant* and *redound*, but not immediately obvious in *abound* and *surround*; indeed, *surround* has suffered the well-meant, confusing attentions of folk-etymology. Relevant to the Greek, Latin, English words and even lighting the way towards a final analysis is the Umbrian *utur*, water.

Aqueous, watery, derives from Latin *aqua*, water, familiar to most of us in *aqua pura*, *aquavitae*, *aquamarine*. *Aqua* is clearly related to the Gothic *ahwa*, a river (compare the synonymous OS and OHG *aha*) and to OHG *ouwa*, a water-meadow, and to OE *ēā*, water, a stream, surviving in the *ea* of English dialect; it is also related to OIr *uisce*, E *whiskey*, as above.

L *aqua* and the Celtic words, however, are not certainly related to E *water* and *wet*, nor to L *unda* and Gr *hudōr*. We have, therefore, two main groups, which I think rest upon one foundation. Is there any evidence for this supposition? I believe, not assert, that the evidence does go to suggest that only a dogmatist would care to asseverate the total absence of kinship.

The authorities seem, on balance, to admit the following facts and theories:

The Celtic *au-* (*av-*) is akin to L *aqua*;

L *aqua* apparently derives from the Indo-European root *akw-*;

L *unda* is a nasalized extension or enlargement of the IE root *ud-*, water, as in the Sanskrit *undáti*, the waters spread out (singular *unátti*)—probably cognate is the Lettish *údens*, water;

G *hudōr* represents *hud-ōr*, with *hud* either an aspirated variation of IE *ud-* or for *wud-*;

E *water* has root *wat-* or *wet-*, themselves variants of IE *wad-* or *wed-*; *was-* and *wed-* were originally *uad-* and *ued-*;

(With a less general assent) the IE *ud-* appears to be an extension of an ultimate IE root *u-*, water, wet—a theory that would open the gates to L *umidus* and Gr *hugros*, moist, along with all the other *u-* terms, a theory I regard, not as necessarily incorrect (although I do rather doubt its correctness) but as irrelevant;

L *amnis*, a river, may represent, not *apnis* (*ap*+-*nis*: *ap*-+ extension -*n*-+declension-indicator -*i*-+nominative ending -*s*) but *abnis* (*ab*-+-*nis*);.............. ... ...

Albanian *uje*, variant *uja*, plural *ujna*, belongs to the *hudōr-unda* group;

Such -*p*- forms, not necessarily of identical origin, as OPrussian *ape*, a brook, and *apus*, a water-spring, the Germanic -*apa* (OHG -*affa*) in Personal Names, and the Gr -*apia* in regional names, and Rumanian *apa*, water, hence such -*p*- forms as Lettish *upe*, Lithuanian *ùpe*, water, must be taken into account.

Those -*p*- words can very easily lead to trouble, for whereas Rumanian *apa* apparently derives from L *aqua* and whereas the other *ap*- words seem to be, somehow, akin to the OIr *aba* (therefore also to L *aqua*), the *up*- words suggest kinship with the words deriving from IE *ud-*.

I now pose a theory or two and adduce certain 'water' (or 'wet') and 'river' words without clarifying their relevancy: I

lack the space—I wish to start several frantic hares—and I feel
that an analysis of the ramifications would suit *Mediterranean*
very much better than they would a Christmas card:

L *aqua* perhaps stands for **uaqua* or **wakwa*: *ua-(wa-)*+
formative *-kw(-q-)*+*-a*, with root **ua-*, ?ultimately **u-*.

To IE **uad-*, **wad-*, and **ued-*, **wed-*, we must add **wud-*,
for Gr *hudōr* could well derive from **wudōr*.

The *-k-* variation attested by Lett *aka*, a water-spring, and
Hittite *eku-*, to drink, and dubiously Tokharian *yoko*, (a) thirst,
should perhaps be aligned with certain OE and ON *-g-* words
that, relevant to the 'water' theme, are here omitted.

An odd variation of the Celtic *ab-*, *av-*, *aw-* forms perhaps
occurs in the Breton *aud*, bank of river or shore of sea.

Basque affords us several entertaining possibilities. For
instance, *uhin*, a wave, and its variants *uhain* and *auhin* curi-
ously resemble L *unda* (? a metathesis for **udna*) and the
Sanskrit genitive *udnas* and the Albanian plural *ujna*; *auaia*
perhaps accidentally recalls the Celtic words in *au-*, but then, I
suspect that Basque, despite its African-type protheses and its
Caucasian affinities, has either a Celtic origin or a potent
Celtic admixture or coloration; to the IE *u-*, with extensions
ua-, *ue-*, *uu-*, the Basque *ui-* of *uial* or *uiol*, a torrent, floods of
water, is startlingly (not, I fear, accidentally) similar; *ur*,
occasionally *hur*, water, in compounds often *u-*, could, without
ingenuity, be related to both Gr *hudōr* and E *water*; only *à
titre de curiosité*, *urandi* (for *ur handi*), a river, is literally 'great
water'.

With IE *uad-*, *ued-*, compare Arabic *wādī*, a river, a river-
bed, and the variant *oued* or *wed*.

The probable Mediterranean origin of *water* receives partial
confirmation from at least one or two of the following Egyptian
words:

åuu, a marsh, a swamp;

åu, a river—compare the Celtic *au-* forms listed above;

år, *aur*, a river; perhaps better transliterated *'io'r*;

åbh, moist, wet;

åitchhu, marshes, swamps, marshy lands;

åtr (better *'iotr*), further vocalized as *atru* (*'iotru*), with

variant *åtur*, a river (? for **watr*, **watru*, **watur*)—perhaps
compare *åtru*, to pour out.

Finally, and again as a mere curiosity, Nahuatl or Aztec
offers a parallel both to such IE forms as *apa*, *ape*, and to the
Sanskrit locative *udan*; to wit, *apan*, occurring in Aztec *Xalapan*
(the Mexican town *Jalapa*, whence *jalap*): *xalli*, sand+*apan*, in
the water. As the Amerindians came from Asia, an Indo-
European survival in Aztec is not so very wildly improbable.
To impute an accidental resemblance is not inevitably the
sensible thing to do.

So far, I lack enough evidence to enable me to declare that
the two basic IE groups of words meaning 'water' are ultimately
identical. But I do think they will probably turn out to be
identical.

SOME ASPECTS OF ETYMOLOGY[1]

Etymology, Greek *etumología*, literally means 'an account of the true'—that is, of the true, especially the original, form and meaning of a word: *etum-*, stem of *etumos*, true + the connective *-o-* + *-logía*, from *logos*, word, account, discourse, and even thought and, as in *logic*, reasoning; an account of the *etymons* or true origins of words, whether individually or collectively: hence the art and science of ascertaining the original forms and meanings of one word or of many. That etymology is a science, no one will deny; that it is also an art, far too many deny.

By the way, it is convenient to restrict the term *etymon* to the original word in its entirety and to apply *root*, *radical* or *base* to the unchangeable core of the etymon concerned. But three cautions must be stated: the first is that *etymons* and *roots* exist at various historical or linguistic levels; the second, that the root is often identical with the etymon: the third, that many words, especially nouns and verbs, have two stems—certain Greek and Latin verbs have three or even four stems—and I'm not talking about those anomalous verbs which have had their conjugation built up from different roots, as, for instance, the (je) *vais*, (j') *allais*, (j)*irai* of the French verb for 'to go', and the three unrelated roots that form the conjugation of the English *be, is, was*. Perhaps an example or two will help. The etymon of *cow* is Old English *cū*, which is both etymon and root. But the Indo-European root of *cow* must have had some such form as **gwō-* or **gwū-* or **gwōu-* becoming *gwou*, for we must account for the cognate Sanskrit *go* and Scandinavian *ko*. English *crime* goes back to Latin *crimen*, with root *crim-* [creem]; but the oblique stem of *crimen* is *crimin-*, seen in our *criminal*. Then take the Latin verb 'to see': Medieval *vidēre*, Classical *uidēre*, root *uid-* [weed], ML *vīd-* [veed], seen in our pro*vide*. But the present participle *uīdens, vīdens*, has oblique stem *uīdent-, vīdent-*, as in our pro*vident*. And the past participle *uīsus, vīsus*, has stem *uīs-, vīs-*, as in our *vision* and *proviso*.

In those examples I have scamped, not distorted, the evidence. One could discourse for an hour, two hours, a day, on the ramifications of English *cow* or those of Latin *uidēre*. But I'm no sadist.

As you know, *etymology* might be defined as the history of change—the changes in a word or in a group of words or, again, in a vast corpus of words. If languages did not change, there could be no *native* etymology, which would then be reduced to a consideration of the cognates in other languages and of the probable Indo-European root. But, everywhere and in many diverse ways, all languages change—or have changed. And, by the way, it is foolish to speak of *dead* languages. Ancient Greek lives on in Modern Greek; Classical Latin in Italian; both Classical and Vulgar Latin in French; Hebrew, though far less vitally, in Yiddish; Sanskrit in Hindi and in Hindustani; Ancient Egyptian in Coptic, itself akin to Ethiopian. Hittite and Tokharian do not lack modern kindred. Even Basque has a dimly discernible ancestor.

To return to our mutations. The changes are of two kinds: in form and in meaning. Besides, every language borrows—or at the least tends to borrow—words from abroad and then either to discard native words that are synonymous or to narrow their meanings. As Professor John W. Clark, of the University of Minnesota, has remarked in his article 'Etymology' in the 1954 recension of *The Encyclopedia Americana*, 'the English-speaking person can hardly read Chaucer or even Shakespeare and can certainly not read *Beowulf* without perceiving that some changes have occurred; and even the relatively incurious and unread can hardly help observing, and wondering at least a little about, such facts as the occasional formal resemblances between words of different meanings (e.g., *cow*, noun, and *cow*, verb) and between words of similar meanings in different languages (e.g., English *beef*, French *boeuf*), and, conversely, the formal differences between words of related meanings (e.g., *cow* and *beef*) and between different meanings of the same word —meanings sometimes co-existent (e.g., *interest*, "fascination" and "income") and sometimes not (e.g., *usury*—now "illegal interest", but formerly "any interest").'

Since languages change, they tend, within any one language-family, to change in much the same way; and all languages whatsoever, irrespective of family relationship, tend to change in certain ways—for instance, they must keep pace with the civilizations they serve, and they borrow from other languages. One's solution of the problems caused by, and involved in, all change, whether operative in any language as a whole or only in its etymology, depends for its success upon the amount and worth of the information gained from research in fields where 'the following kinds of data are available', as John W. Clark,[1] from whom I forthwith quote, has postulated:

'(1) Considerable masses of at least roughly datable documents yielding a fairly continuous record of the language throughout its history; (2) relevant records of languages from which any considerable number of words have been borrowed; (3) relevant records of the other languages of the same linguistic family. These several kinds of data,' he adds, 'are available in sufficient quantities for only relatively few languages, pre-eminent among which are the languages of the Indo-European family.'

Since the rest of this paper concerns that linguistic family, perhaps I might, even though the generalities of the subject are familiar to you, do worse than risk one or two more generalities.

Indo-European is a far better name than either *Aryan*, which is vague and misleading, or *Indo-Germanic*, which is still more misleading and inadequate. The Indo-European languages have descended, and in descending have increasingly diverged, from a single language or, some of them, from one or two extremely important dialects of that language, which we call either Primitive Indo-European or simply Indo-European and which was probably spoken at least as early as 4000 B.C. You will, in passing, notice that we have pushed ever farther back the 'chronological frontiers' of all languages and indeed of all language: for instance, where formerly we used to assign the ulterior limit of Sanskrit to about 1500 B.C., we now assign it to

[1] Loc. cit.

about 2000 B.C. Perhaps I might also recall that the chief branches of the Indo-European family are these: Indic, notably Sanskrit and modern Hindi; Iranian, especially Persian and Afghan; Greek; Latin and its Romance descendants, Italian, Spanish, Portuguese, French, Rumanian; Tokharian—the two dialects or, maybe, parallels; Celtic—the long extinct Gaulish, the recently extinct Cornish, Breton, Welsh, Irish, (Scots) Gaelic, Manx; Slavic, especially Russian; Baltic, e.g. Lithuanian; Armenian; Albanian; and Germanic—the extinct Gothic, German, Dutch, Old Frisian, English, the Scandinavian languages.

More than the Chinese, and more than the Semitic and the Hamitic, the Indo-European languages are, as a group, notable —all, in some respects, and some, in all respects, unique—in the following ways: their historical importance; the wealth of their literatures; the sweeping and remarkably diverse changes they have experienced. Moreover, their inter-relations have been studied more intensively than those of any other linguistic family.

The cultural or civilizational importance of the Indo-European languages combines with the generally high level of intelligence among the speakers of these languages to account for the complexities of Indo-European etymology, but also to supply an astounding quantity and diversity of evidence. If the complexity has caused numerous problems, it has also—and inevitably—presented us with numerous clues. Professor Clark has noted the astonishing fact that 'the English verb *was* and the -*er*- in *Canterbury* go back to the same Indo-European base'. But hardly less astonishing is the fact that English *am*, *is*, *are* belong to the same Indo-European stem as Latin *sum*, Greek *eimi*, I am—to Greek *esti*, Latin *est*, German *ist*, he is, wherein the -*t* indicates the Third Person Singular—to Old English *sind*, Gothic *sind*, Latin *sunt*, Sanskrit santi [sahn'tee], they are; to the -*sent* in *absent* and *present*, and the *ent*- in *entity*; more distantly yet no less certainly, to the *et*- in *etymology* (a story I tell elsewhere) and also to *sooth*, true, real, from a hypothetical Primitive Germanic root *santh*-, with which, rather obviously, compare the just mentioned Sanskrit *santi*, they are, and the

Sanskrit combining-form *sant-*, existing, real. All those various and apparently very diverse forms derive ultimately from a Sanskrit root **es-*, to be. In fairness I should like to add several tiny clues that etymologists do not always mention: to Attic Greek *eimi*, and Thessalian Greek *emmi*, I am, there exists an arresting cognate in Old English—*ĕom*, I am; the *-nd-* and *-nt-* forms are not necessarily due to nasalization, as such, and they constitute a predominant feature in the formation of present participles.

But etymology has not always been so intelligent; or rather, etymologists only in the latter part of the eighteenth century began to acquire the knowledge requisite for an intelligently comparative study of the Indo-European languages, much of the credit being due to an Englishman, Sir William Jones (1746–94). Britons, it might be remembered, have done more and better work in philology in general and etymology in particular than most foreigners and too many Britons will admit; and in this excellence I associate Americans. Before Jones and, except among a few scholars, for thirty-or-so years after his death, etymology merited the definition, attributed to Voltaire: 'A science in which the consonants are of very little importance, and the vowels of none at all'. Even Noah Webster, who should have known better, had several exceedingly odd ideas; yet, in the 1820's, Jacob Grimm and Rasmus Rask were formulating 'laws' of the utmost importance, 'laws' notably supplemented in the 1870's by Karl Verner. With the more recent 'giants of philology' (as I once saw a newspaper describe them) it would be invidious—and probably dangerous—to deal.

What philologists in general and etymologists in particular have come to realize is that, despite the rather numerous *apparent* exceptions and anomalies, philology and, although perhaps slightly less, etymology rank as sciences precisely because (again to quote John W. Clark) 'they proceed on the assumptions, justified by the results, on which all science proceeds—to wit, that nothing happens without cause and that the same cause under the same conditions will always bring about the same results'. The doctrinal position is now such that nine

out of ten philologists hold that if a proposed etymology of any
Indo-European word fails to conform to the 'laws' of *sound*-
correspondence, that particular etymology is almost certainly
wrong. And at least one philologist further holds that meaning
is entirely and always subordinate to sound; by which, I
presume, he intends to say, 'meaning is always subordinate to
that inseparable duad, sound-and-form'.

The word he selects is *dream*. John W. Clark's semantic
explanation of this word is based upon the very reasonable
assumption that the sense of the Primitive Indo-European
etymon from which descend both the Old English *drēam*,
primarily 'joy', secondarily 'music', and the Old Norse *draumr*,
almost solely 'dream', was 'sound' or 'noise'. 'The main Old
English meaning, "joy", presumably results from [some such
development as] "sound, sound of merriment, festival music,
festival activity, pleasure, joy"; the Old Norse meaning, from
some such development as "sound, noise, rumor, lying rumor,
lie, deception, deceptive vision, vision, dream".' He concludes
thus: 'The Modern English *form* is apparently Old English in
origin; the *meaning*, Old Norse. This is very far from improbable
considering (1) the close genetic relation between English
and Norse, (2) their mutual intelligibility. *ca.* 900 A.D., when
most of the Norse settlements in England occurred, and (3) the
virtual blending of the language of Scandinavian settlers in
England with the language of their English neighbors.'

But to revert to *sound*-correspondences. The 'laws' governing
them should not be prosecuted beyond the limits of good, as
opposed to mere common, sense. We do not, for instance, know
precisely how Primitive Indo-European was pronounced, nor
precisely how Sanskrit or even Greek was pronounced. Take
Greek! There has been a controversy raging about the pronunciation of χ (*khai*): is its phonetic value merely that of a
strongly aspirated *k* (the old, long-held, not yet disproved
opinion) or does χ represent a barely audible division *k-h*? Then
there are οἱ, *hoi*, the masculine plural of the definite article,
and οἱ, *hoi*, the masculine plural of the relative pronoun 'who,
which'. That is the old pronunciation: the modern school holds
that, to take a phrase we all of us know, *hoi polloi*, the many,

should be pronounced *hwah polwah*, although some of the moderns hold that *hoi* becomes *hwah* only in the relative pronoun, their reason—an excellent reason—being that obviously *hwa* stands very much closer to our *who*, Early Middle English *hwo*, Old English *hwā* [hwah] than *hoi* does, and also to the Latin relative. Latin, by the way, has its problems too.

Here we may interpose a few words on Semantics or the so-called 'science' of meaning: the science that treats of the nature, the inter-relationships and especially the developments and changes in the meanings of words and phrases and also (though I've heard no one remark the fact) in the turns of phrase and clause and sentence. By itself, *Semantics* (a word plural in form but singular in construction) is not enough, but, as Professor Weekley has often shown, it is a valuable ally, in that it sometimes provides a clue, notably as to the direction—e.g., the language—in which to search for the origin of a troublesome word. Sense-identities occur rarely, but sense-contiguities and sense-parallels occur frequently.

To be dogmatic for a moment, one may postulate the following axioms:

(1) If between a Modern English word and (say) a Hittite word, there exist correspondences in sound, form, meaning, those words are akin, as e.g. *water* and Hittite *watar* [wahtar]. Despite the arresting correspondence, only a linguistic lunatic would derive *water* from *watar*; the correspondence merely illustrates the fact that Hittite is in some way related to the Indo-European languages.

(2) If, however, we set the English adjective *lucent* beside Latin *lucent-* [loo-kent], the oblique stem of *lucens* [loo-kens], the present participle of *lucēre* [loo-kay'-ree], to be light, to shine, we know that, there, we have the origin. (By the way, compare Latin *lux*, light, with Hittite *lukzi*, lights up.)

(3) The *lucent* example shows that, providing both the form and the meaning of a word agree, the sound need not exactly agree. For English there is a compulsive reason for this: the letters representing the long vowels denote certain phonetic values that are the same in all languages—except English. Britons and Americans just have to be different! Their inde-

pendence is, in most ways, an admirable characteristic: but in a comparative study of language it is rather a nuisance. This linguistic characteristic forms one of the major difficulties blocking the way to a reformed spelling.

(4) If two words agree in form and sound, yet differ somewhat in sense, that sense-discrepancy has to be explained; it cannot be allowed to outweigh the form- and sound-correspondences, provided there be sufficient evidence to link the modern word with the proposed original. Take the modern slangy adjective *rum*, meaning 'odd, strange, (in short) queer', and the sixteenth-to-seventeenth century adjective *rum*, meaning 'fine, excellent'. The modern meaning is very different from the old. But the semantic change can be quite easily explained: the old adjective *rum* was a term used by the London underworld, and its opposite was *queer*. Now, the underworld senses of *rum* were 'fine, excellent, costly; briefly, superior or even the best'; of *queer*, 'of bad quality, cheap, cheap and nasty; briefly, inferior or even downright bad'. But what seemed good to the underworld might seem very bad, because extremely disadvantageous, to the honest citizen. The two adjectives, therefore, are etymologically identical. (But this *rum* is merely a homonym of *rum* the potent spirit.)

Thus we arrive at homonyms, and by the term I understand words that are spelt and pronounced alike but have different meanings and are of different origin, not such homophones as *b-o-a-r* and *b-o-r-e*. A good example is afforded by that *policy*, akin to *police* and *politics*, which comes from Greek *polis*, a city, and that other, the insurance *policy*, which comes from Italian *polizza*, which, by aphesis, comes from Medieval Latin *apodixa*, itself from Greek *apodeixis*, proof. There, no doubt exists; but certain supposed homonyms probably derive from a common origin; one must be on guard against excessive differentiation. More than once it will be found that the fact of common origin has been overlooked simply because of that *I-him* relationship, more ambitiously described as the subjective-objective relationship, which occurs in so many words and even in syntax. *His* success perhaps means my failure, *his* victory my disaster, *his* good my ill, as we saw in the rogue's sixteenth-to-seventeenth century and the honest man's nineteenth-to-twentieth century interpretation of the adjective *rum*. I put forward this suggestion in the hope that, one day, someone will make a thorough study of homonyms.

Most of those aspects of etymology have been fully treated elsewhere; several of them, indeed, by many scholars. I should like to pass to a few aspects deserving, I believe, far more attention—and much greater care—than they have received. I can deal with them only very briefly, hence very inadequately. Please regard them as, in the better sense of that word, provocations.

The first aspect is the historical. In general, too little recourse has been had to, and too little verification has been made by, history. On the negative side, however, history has not been neglected, especially where anachronism is suspected; nor has scholarship failed when it needs to determine the order and the nature of successive borrowings of the same word, as, for instance—it is John Clark's instance—*dish, desk, dais, disk, discus*. (Here I wish to make it clear that several of the shortcomings of etymology result, not from deficiencies in the etymologists themselves, but from lack of time: for that etymologist who 'loves' his work, and nobody should be one unless he does, life is far too short.)

No; I wish here to urge upon you the value—often, indeed, the necessity—of going to history for clues as well as corroborations. With history I link the physical framework of history: geography: and, above all, historical geography, which is of primary importance to the etymologist. Of history itself, the most helpful kind is that which concerns itself with civilization or, rather, civilizations or, as is now the fashion to say, with cultures. In this sense, *culture* has recently been defined as 'the concepts, habits, skills [what we used to call 'crafts'], arts, instruments, institutions, etc. [including, presumably, customs] of a given people at a given time'. (*Webster's New World Dictionary of the American Language*, College Edition, 1952.) If any of you thinks this definition the apotheosis of the letter as distinct from the spirit of civilization, I shall not invite him, much less *her*, to 'coffee for one': apart from the mention of 'concepts', it ignores religion and philosophy: it refers to the arts, yet omits literature; it implies mind, yet almost entirely excludes spirit, without which mankind would be doomed.

But we were speaking of the value of history and geography. To take a shamelessly egotistic example, I could not have solved the problem inherent in the etymology of *tarot* (the *tarot* cards used in fortune-telling) without some knowledge of the history of the Gypsies. I sha'n't bore you with it, for I have briefly told the story in *From Sanskrit to Brazil*, a title that caused a very good scholar to imply, although he didn't in so many words say, that he thought it damn' silly.

History, I need hardly emphasize, is implicit in all philology; nor have philologists underestimated its general importance. Just now and again I find myself wishing that its importance in the lexicography of languages not their own were less sporadically recognized, and utilized, by them. At the moment I'm thinking of Greek and Latin, about which I should like to make two or three extremely brief and doubtless unsatisfactory remarks.

In dealing with Greek, one should transliterate correctly and, in several instances, complementarily. That seems obvious; yet how very seldom is it done! In one or two dictionaries you will not even find the Greek characters transliterated; in most, you have the transliteration but not the Greek, and in one respect the transliteration is misleading, that of *ch* instead of *kh* for χ, and in another, affecting that group of four combinations which we might call 'the nasalizing-*gamma* quartette', not only misleading but wrong. The table is easy:

$$γγ, \text{ gamma gamma} = ng;$$
$$γχ, \text{ gamma kappa} = nk;$$
$$γξ, \text{ gamma xi} = nx;$$
$$\text{and } γχ, \text{ gamma khai} = nkh.$$

To transliterate gamma gamma as *gg*, gamma kappa as *gk*, gamma xi as *gx* and gamma khai as *gch* is, for the non-Grecian, even more misleading than to put the Greek characters without transliteration. Examples that are relevant to *English* may help us: Greek κλάγγη [klang-ē], a confused or inarticulate cry, especially if shrill, apparently spelt k-l-a-g-g-ē, should be transliterated 'klang-ē' or 'k-l-a-g-g-ē, pronounced *klang-ē*', for only thus can the non-Grecian see its kinship to English *clang*. The Simple Future κλάγξω [*klanx-ō*], I shall shriek, exemplifies γξ, gamma xi, although a better example is afforded by λύγξ, *lunx*, our *lynx*; the combination γκ, gamma kappa, appears, for instance, in λυγκός, *lunkos*, the genitive of *lunx*; and γχ, gamma khai, in λόγχη, *lonkhē*, lance or javelin, literally 'the long thing', the Greek word being thus seen to be kin to English *long*.

For Latin, I shall confine myself to a couple of scriptural-phonetic points: these concern the letters we call *i* and *j*, and those we call *u* and *v*. On *i* and *j* I quote probably the best all-round British Classical scholar of this century: the lamented Alexander Souter, who, in *A Glossary of Later Latin*, says, 'The letter *J*, which is really an elongated *I*, is first used in cursive writing to indicate an initial *I*, but in the semi-vocalic sense is not used until about A.D. 800 and then only in South Italy and Spain'. Never, in referring to Latin before that date, spell with a *j* a word beginning with *i*; and remember that even after that date it is pronounced approximately *y*, not as our English *j*; remember also that only English pronounces *j* as we pronounce it. If you see *i-a-c-ē-r-e*, to lie down, written with a *j*, it is still pronounced *yă-kay'-re*.

As for the letters *u* and *v*, there are several points to notice. Small *v*, as it is printed, is a reduction to lower-case of upper-case or capital *V*, as it is printed; in Classical and even in Late Latin (roughly A.D. 180–600) capital *V* was the way capital *U* was written, as you have doubtless seen in inscriptions; the displacement, in Latin, of *u* by *v* does not precede the darkest Middle Ages—that it took place *then*, we can deduce from Old French. The importance of writing and pronouncing Classical and Late Latin words beginning with *u* as *u*, pronounced *oo*, is greater in etymology than some people seem to realize. Take Latin *uinum* [wee'-num], meaning primarily 'wine', secondarily 'vine': that, the correct, pronunciation links the word not only with our *wine* but also with Greek *oinos*, which, if pronounced *wah'-nos*, does away with the need to postulate that the word was originally written with a digamma—a letter that, discarded before Classical Greek existed, has the form of a sans-serif capital *F* but is pronounced like our *w*. But the Medieval Latin pronunciation *vinum* [vee'-noom] accounts for French *vin*; *vin*, of course, does not form the origin of our *vine*, which comes from Old French *vine*, whence Modern French *vigne*; OF *vine* derives from Medieval Latin *vinea* [vee-nay'-ă], the vine, from Latin *uīnea*, oo-ee-nay'-a, that is wee-nay'-a, properly the feminine of the adjective *uīneus*, wee-nay'-ooss; with *uīnea* [wee-nay'-ă] compare the synonymous Greek *oiné* [wah'-nay]. By the way, the word variously represented in Indo-European by *oinos* [wah'-nos], *uinum* [wee'-noom], *vin*, *vine*, *vēne* [way'-ne] (the Albanian form) and *gini* [ghee'-nee] (the Armenian), occurs also in Semitic languages, for example Hebrew *jajin* [yah'-yeen], and in the Hamitic. But I sha'n't weary you with my theory on the subject of such 'Mediterranean words', as Boisacq calls them; nor shall I expatiate upon my opinion that, in English etymology, Greek is rather more important than Latin—and that Latin is indispensable.

Latin has, in one sense, more ramifications than Greek: whereas the modern descendant of Greek is Modern Greek, the modern descendant of Latin is the entire group of Romance languages—Italian; Spanish; Catalan and Provençal; Portuguese; French; and Rumanian.

The Romance languages present a very tricky problem in chronology. If, however, you keep in mind the 'colonies' or settlements founded or made by Roman soldiers, camp-followers and more reputable traders, you will not go far wrong, especially if you remember that trade sometimes preceded conquest or military occupation. Here you have language in a phase where Historical Geography will help you considerably. Every Romance language has existed in the three phases—Old (or Ancient), Medieval, Modern—with the proviso that Old Italian is better known as Late, and Early Medieval, Latin. Unfortunately, the records of the earliest phase of two or three Romance languages are meagre.

Complicating the problem of Romance chronology is that of

Celtic chronology. Of the thorny subject of Celtic elements in
Old Germanic, I shall say nothing, for the most compulsive of
all reasons: I know nothing about it. I know almost as little
about the Celtic elements in Romance—apart, at least, from
the Celtic influence on Latin, especially on Silver Latin (*ca.*
A.D. 14–180) and Late Latin. The question of the Latin element in Celtic as a whole needs to be restated: that of the Celtic
element in Latin, from early Republican days until the end of
(say) the fifteenth century, demands a comprehensive study and
perhaps a glossary. But then, we further need at least two comparative dictionaries of Celtic: one from the earliest days until
(say) 1500, the other for modern times.

The trouble is that, of all the fields of Indo-European philology, the most neglected is that of Celtic—the most neglected,
that is, in proportion to the wealth and importance of Celtic in
general and in particular. The number of British chairs in
Celtic—although this stricture applies more to the Dominions
than to these islands—would disgrace the seating accommoda-
tion in the foyer of a third-rate hotel.

Celtic falls into three periods: Old, Middle, Modern. Irish
and Welsh possess a very fair amount of lexical evidence for all
three; Gaulish, for only one—the Old; Cornish, to which
Breton is so closely related, died, as an *active* language, *ca.* 1800.
Irish and Gaelic (or, if you wish, Scottish Gaelic) are very
closely linked; the most independent and the least studied of
modern Celtic languages is Manx, spoken by a proud people in
an island long existing in isolation— a language *not*, as several
dictionaries state, 'almost extinct'. One of its most interesting
features, and philologically its perhaps most important, is this:
if you take the usually presumed Old Celtic root as the norm,
you find that whereas Gaelic and Irish in one or other of its
phases, and Welsh in one or other of *its* phases, possess or
possessed a word varying in an easily recognizable form; that
whereas the Cornish and Breton words, though usually not
quite so obviously akin, bear resemblances at least cousinly—
when they bear any at all; that whereas Gaulish words may,
superficially, look somewhat outlandish; the Manx word, more
often than not, exhibits differences explainable only in the light

of vowel-changes and consonantal alterations or, at least, shifts ; yet the Manx word often illuminates the apparently Cimmerian gulf between the Common Celtic root and the (say) Latin root or, better, the Common Indo-European root. Nor, in these random remarks, am I forgetting that whereas Breton, Cornish, Welsh belong to the south-western or Brythonic (or Brittonic) branch, Irish, Gaelic, Manx belong to the Goidelic branch; or that Gaulish stands rather apart, perhaps for geographical reasons (the language having been spoken very far afield, even in parts of Asia Minor), certainly for its structure, probably for its chronology, Gaulish having either fallen into disuse or perhaps disintegrated—that is dispersed—somewhere about A.D. 500. The chief point I wish to make is that most philologists, even some of the Celtic philologists, very rarely, when they are comparing one Celtic language with another, still more when they are comparing a (say) Romance language with Celtic, deign to adduce a Manx word. I feel very strongly on this subject of Manx; perhaps because of my abysmal ignorance.

One thing, however, I do know or, at any rate, *seem* to know. In the Celtic languages, one cannot escape the impression that here is a speech, here a vocabulary, very intimately related to mountains, high hills, the uplands: and that impression has not arisen as 'wisdom after the event', based upon the attractive interpretation of the word *Celt* as 'man of the mountains'. That is a tempting theory, because, like so many other ancient racial designations, the term existed as a plural before there was a singular: so perhaps the Celts were, after all, originally 'the people of the mountains', in opposition, it is possible, to 'the men of the plains', especially of the great Tigris–Euphrates basin, so often called 'the cradle of civilization'.

After all that haziness, I somewhat belatedly hasten to make a few casual remarks upon two pairs of 'mystery words'—that is, words of unknown origin—and finally to issue a grave warning.

The mysterious pairs are *lad* and *lass*, and *boy* and *girl*. I cannot solve them for you, but I may be able to set you on a couple of likely paths.

Boy and *girl* seem to be as far apart as, except for the suffix of the second pair, *brother* and *sister*. *Lad* and *lass*, on the contrary, probably have a common origin, much as those two disguised compounds *lord* and *lady* have a common origin. The usual guess that *lass* derives from an Old Norse word meaning 'weak' or 'idle' strikes me as feeble and the usual assumption that *lass* is independent of *lad* fails to convince me. On the other hand I like the suggestion that *lad*, Middle English *ladde*, derives from late Old English *-ladda*, occurring only as a second element in place-name and by-name compounds, an element akin to the Old English element *-led*, sprout, as in the name *Sumerled* [soo'-mer-led], literally 'summer sprout', and to the Gothic element *-lauths*, sprout, as in *juggalauths* [yoong'-gă-lauths], young man, literally 'young sprout or growth'. This etymology postulates for *lad* the entirely suitable basic sense 'young sprout or growth'—compare the phrases *young sprig* and *a sprig of the nobility* and, more vaguely and remotely, *young things*. If you accept that etymology for *lad* and further accept the probability that *lass* derives from *lad*, you are forced to accept some such derivation as *lad—lad-ess—la'esss—lass*. Although I lack the evidence to corroborate that derivation, I think that it may well exist: after all, our linguistic records are, at many points, far from complete.

Boy and *girl*, however, are obviously independent, the one of the other. *Boy*, Middle English *boie*, is probably akin to East Frisian *boi*, a young gentleman, perhaps also to German *Bube* [boo'-bŭ], a knave, and Old Norse *bufi* [boo'-fee], a rogue— compare semantically, although in reverse, English *knave* from Old English *cnafe* [knah'-fa], akin to German *Knabe* [knah'-be], a boy. Those few details have been well known since late in the nineteenth century, but the lexicographers should, I think, have made it clear, even though it is obvious, that the comparison of English *boy* with German *bube*, Middle High German *buobe* [boo'-o-be], Old Norse *bufi*, is probably valid only for the first element *bu-* [boo]. That element *bu-* is important, for it at least suggests an Indo-European stem and a Latin cognate, perhaps a Greek cognate—and certainly a semantic parallel in *lad*. The Indo-European stem, I'd say, is *pu-* [poo-], occurring perhaps in Sanskrit and in Latin and, with vowel-change, in Greek; with Germanic alteration *bu-*. The basic sense of Indo-European **pu-* would be 'to grow' or 'growth', specialized as 'young growth'. But can we substantiate that airy proposal? Sanskrit has *pumán* [poo'-mahn], a man: by a man we tend to understand a man in full growth, yet before he begins to lose his strength and energy. Latin has two significant words, in which the idea of growth is manifest: *pubes* [poo'-base], one who is physically adult, at least essentially; and *puer* [poo'-er], a boy, 'a *growing* male', literally a *grow*-er', the *-er* being agential. (*Puella* [poo'-ella] derives from *puer* and consists of stem *pu-+-ella*, feminine diminutive suffix, *puella* being 'the little female *grow*-er'; *puellus* doesn't help, for it has been re-fashioned upon *puella*.) What, then, is the Greek word? *Pais* [pice], a boy, *pu-* having, by 'popular' vocalism, become *pa-* [pah]; *-is* being a masculine suffix; the original form may have been *pa-wis*[1]—*pá-+*digamma+-*is*. If we accept the Indo-European and Latin kinship, we necessarily abandon the 'boy'-'rogue' semantic parallel, which clearly is neither essential nor even relevant.

Thus we reach that difficult word *girl*. The Middle English forms *girle* (gheer'-le], *gerle* [gher'-le], *gurle* [ghoor'-le], meaning a young person of either sex, but, especially towards the end of the period, mostly a girl, apparently derive from Old English *-gyrl* [gheer'l], recorded in *gyrlgyden* [gheerl'-gheeden], virgin goddess. Perhaps akin to the Old English word is the Low German *gör* [gher] or *göre* [gher'-e], a young person of either sex, but that doesn't take us very far. The semantic approach may help, because one basic sense—as in *lad* and *boy*—appears to be 'young person, growing person, of either sex', and another, still more fundamental, sense appears to be 'growing thing' (the generalization or abstraction would be 'growth'). If, for the purposes of discussion, we admit that semantic premiss, we look for lexical and phonetic evidence: and, looking, we find, in Old English, the rare word *gyr* [gheer], a fig-tree, and, in Southern English dialect, *girlopp* [gher'-lop], a lout, and, even more revealing, *girls* [gherls], primrose blooms.

---

[1] I owe *pais* to Ernout & Meillet.

For those three terms, as for the semantic suggestion, I am indebted to *Webster's New World Dictionary of the American Language* (College Edition, 1952), which also put me on what seems to be the right track for *lad*. I used to think, nor am I convinced that I was wrong in thinking, that *girl* might be ultimately kin to Greek κόρη, *korē*, pronounced *ko-ray*, a young girl, the root being *kor-* and the word being merely the feminine of κόρος, *koros*, a child, an adolescent; the apparently later sense 'a shoot, a sprout' may, in fact, have been the earlier. The Indo-European root has been postulated as *ker-*: compare the poetic κέλωρ, *kelōr*, son, for *κέρωρ, *kerōr*; the suffix -ωρ, -*ōr*, is akin to Latin -*er*, as in *puer* [poo'-er]. The words *koros* and *korē* would mean 'young *grow*-er', respectively male and female. Suppose we grant the Indo-European stem *ker-*, to grow, can we link it to our *girl*, Old English *gyrl-* [gheerl]? The final *l* is a suffix, probably here, as so often elsewhere, short for -*el*, fundamentally a diminutive, but with the diminutive force either lost or exceedingly vague. That still leaves us with the necessity of equating *ker-* with *ger-*: but is that more difficult than equating, as better philologists than I have equated, *ker-* with Armenian *ser*, lineage, posterity, and *serim*, I am descended from? And with Latin *crĕ-* or *crē* [cray], as in *creare*, to create, (fundamentally) to cause to *grow*? Why not also the *ser-* of Latin *serĕre*, stem *ser-*, to sow, a root occurring in several other languages for both 'to sow' and 'to plant'? Now, Latin *crĕ-* or *crē* [cray] may be a metathesis of Indo-European *ker-*. The letter *k* is phonetically equivalent to hard *c*; and what is *g*— that is, hard *g*—but a thickening of hard *c*, hence of *k*? Admit that and you will, however reluctantly, admit the transition, from *ker-* to *ger-* [gher], hence from *kor-*, as in *korē* [ko-ray], a young girl, to *girl*. The vowel-change is, at first thought, a violent one; yet several great philologists, as we have seen, do admit it in Greek *korē* [ko-ray] and Indo-European *ker-*.

But the etymology of *girl*—a word unrecorded before the late thirteenth century—is so obscure that there exists yet another possibility. The late appearance of the word renders unlikely an origin in Greek or Latin.

A famous dictionary calls the pronunciation *gal* 'dialectal and vulgar': yet it has always been, predominantly, an educated and even a society pronunciation. To show you how untrustworthily my mind works I confess that my attention strays to Irish simply because of the Anglo-Irish *girleen*, apparently a blend of the English *girl* and the Anglo-Irish *colleen*.

Now, *colleen* represents Irish c-a-i-l-ĭ-n (pronounced roughly *că-leen*), diminutive of Irish c-a-i-l-e (roughly *că'-'l'ay*), from Early Middle Irish c-a-l-e (roughly *că-lay*)—stem *căl*. *Căl* to *gal* presents an easy and frequent mutation. Perhaps *ca-lay* was, by English ears, apprehended as *cah'-lay*, and then *cah* as *cahr*: which would explain the intrusive *r*. The vowel *ah* might easily, in a period of phonetic and scriptural chaos or, at best, indecision, have been thinned to 'the neutral vowel': which would explain the variants g-*e*-r-l-e, g-*i*-r-l-e, g-*u*-r-l-e.

That, however, is a mere suggestion.

The simple truth is that we lack the evidence to decide upon one of those three theories about the etymology of *girl* at the expense of the other two; nor am I trying to be ingenious. So please regard my disjointed remarks on *lad-lass* and *boy-girl* as what it is the fashion to call an 'interim report'. I've done no exhaustive work upon any of them. Indeed, I am almost content to say 'I don't *know*'.

I shall, however, be well content if I have said enough to insinuate into your minds a partial sympathy with my intolerant attitude towards a statement attributed—wrongly, I feel sure—to Skeat of the still extremely useful etymological dictionary: 'If I cannot solve an etymology in twenty minutes, I give it up'. Many of Skeat's own etymologies must have taken him very much longer than that. He was not impatient: no philologist should be, no etymologist can afford to be. In etymology, it is better to travel than to arrive—not that the arrival fails to bring one a lively gratification.

Yet, because of the fascination of these journeys—a fascination that can be shared at second hand—and the very lively satisfaction, likewise shareable, caused by the arrival, I feel it my solemn duty to warn you, as emphatically as courtesy permits, against etymology. Without cataloguing you into boredom, I shall mention only a few of the very real, and very grave, dangers of engaging in etymology: beside which, Cleopatra was a quickly fading harridan, too soon agèd, for the fascination of etymology *can* never stale, let alone die.

Etymology, you see, calls for the exercise of mind, but also of will: for cool judgement, but also a warm heart: for knowledge of books, but also of mankind: for research into books, but also into life: for a bed-rock of philology, but also a deep top-soil of general culture: for a knowledge of, or at least an unfailing tact in, psychology, but also a wide reading in history: for a combination of well-ordered general knowledge and of well-directed specialized knowledge: that specialized knowledge falling into two parts, a general knowledge of language and its operations, and a particular knowledge of all those branches of philology upon which etymology, if it is not to degenerate into ingenuity on one hand or into fancy on the other, must be based. Advisedly I say 'fancy', 'not 'imagination'. In etymology, imagination, if carefully controlled, will occasionally solve problems that phonetics cannot touch; it must, however, be imagination exercised, not in defiance of philology but within the vast horizons available to even the most formal philology; the trouble is that some people shrink from marching to the horizon, for fear (an early medieval fear) of falling over the world's edge.

Etymology is a perilous subject: for, reach one horizon, you find another equally distant, if not still more remote. One clue leads to another, which yields to another, which *ad-infinitum*s from days to months to years; and often one has to retrace one's steps.

'This way madness lies.' But—to oneself always; to others occasionally—it's a remarkably pleasant madness.

(Delivered, on October 19, 1953, as a paper to the English Seminar of the University of Liverpool.)